Norwegian Minds—
American Dreams

Norwegian Minds— American Dreams

Ethnic Activism among Norwegian-American Intellectuals

Peter Thaler

Newark: University of Delaware Press
London: Associated University Presses

© 1998 by Associated University Presses, Inc.

All rights reserved. Authorization to photocopy items for internal or personal use, or the internal or personal use of specific clients, is granted by the copyright owner, provided that a base fee of $10.00, plus eight cents per page, per copy is paid directly to the Copyright Clearance Center, 222 Rosewood Drive, Danvers, Massachusetts 01923. [0-87413-629-6/98 $10.00 + 8¢ pp, pc.]

Associated University Presses
440 Forsgate Drive
Cranbury, NJ 08512

Associated University Presses
16 Barter Street
London WC1A 2AH, England

Associated University Presses
P.O. Box 338, Port Credit
Mississauga, Ontario
Canada L5G 4L8

The paper used in this publication meets the requirements of the American National Standard for Permanence of Paper for Printed Library Materials Z39.48–1984.

Library of Congress Cataloging-in-Publication Data

Thaler, Peter, 1960–
   Norwegian minds, American dreams / Peter Thaler.
     p. cm.
   Includes bibliographical references (p.   ) and index.
   ISBN 0-87413-629-6 (alk. paper)
   1. Norwegian-American literature—History and criticism. 2. Ethnicity—United States. 3. Norwegian Americans—Intellectual life. 4. Immigrants in literature. I. Title.
PT9131.T43   1998
810.9'83982—DC21
                                              97-19957
                                                  CIP

PRINTED IN THE UNITED STATES OF AMERICA

Contents

Acknowledgments   7

1. Introduction to Norwegian-America and Its Literary Image   11
2. Assailing the Melting Pot—Waldemar Ager   31
3. Simon Johnson: A Chronicler of His Time   44
4. Hans Rønnevik's Answer to the Loyalism Campaign   56
5. Wheat and Potatoes—Ethnic and Religious Differences in O. E. Rølvaag's Immigrant Trilogy   69
6. Preservationist Ideas in Fiction and in Political Discourse   83
7. Reception in the Norwegian-American Community   107
8. Ethnicity, Activism, and Literature—A Conclusion Put into Context   120

Notes   140
Bibliography   147
Index   159

Acknowledgments

IN THIS BOOK, I HAVE TRIED TO COMBINE THE INTERESTS AND approaches of more than one scholarly discipline. The study is about ideas, and ideas do not belong to any one discipline alone. As a consequence, I have consulted with a diverse group of researchers and archivists during the course of this project. At this point, I would like to acknowledge their assistance.

I owe thanks to the staff at various libraries and archives. I received considerable help from the libraries at the Universities of Oslo, Minnesota, and Wisconsin as well as at St. Olaf College and Luther College. Equally important was the assistance given by the State Historical Societies of Minnesota and Wisconsin and, in particular, by the staff at the indispensable Norwegian-American Historical Association under its editor, Odd Lovoll.

Drafts of the manuscript were read by Michael Metcalf, Harald Naess, William Mishler, Rudolph Vecoli, and, above all, Göran Stockenström; their constructive criticism and their encouragement assisted me throughout my research. Tina Thaler and Kurt Goblirsch improved style and language, and the helpful reviewers and editors at the University of Delaware Press and at Associated University Presses provided the final touch. I am glad to be able to acknowledge these contributions.

Norwegian Minds—
American Dreams

1
Introduction to Norwegian-America and Its Literary Image

DURING THE FIRST DECADES OF THE TWENTIETH CENTURY, THE Norwegian-Americans participated in the celebration of three historical events that possessed particular significance for this immigrant community.

In 1905 an old dream came true and Norway reemerged as a genuinely independent country. After centuries of Danish (and later Swedish) domination, Norwegians all over the world rejoiced when Denmark's prince Carl was crowned Haakon VII, King of Norway.

When Norway commemorated the centennial of its liberal Eidsvoll constitution in 1914, thousands of people visited the old country to experience the festive spirit.[1] The immigrant community was prospering. The first years along the frontier had been harsh, but the new Americans eventually established themselves successfully on the prairie. The United States census of 1910 recorded more than one million first- and second-generation Norwegian-Americans, who had built an impressive network of ethnic churches, newspapers, and organizations.[2] Norwegian America was at its peak, and to many observers its future seemed secure.

At the 1925 centennial of the arrival of the "Norwegian Mayflower," as the first ship of Norwegian emigrants to America sometimes has been called, the immigrant community again seemed to present a commanding display of organized institutional strength. President Coolidge honored the celebrating crowds in Minneapolis with his presence, underlining the respect they had won in their new country. The power base of Norwegian culture in America, however, was already eroding. The war, immigration restrictions, and the employment opportunities created by industrialization in Norway drastically reduced the number of new immigrants, severing the lifeline through which this culture received its replenishment. At the same time, the Americanization drive that originated during World War I uncovered the underlying weakness of the immigrant culture. Assimilation had progressed rapidly in the American-born generations, and the pressures of the loyalism campaign induced many more to discard their old-country ways. The impressive numerical strength of the immigrant community and its institutions could no longer hide its inner frailty, and although language is not the only criterion of the vitality of an immigrant culture, it remains indicative that most of the festivities during the centennial were held in English.

The number of Americans who listed Norwegian as their mother tongue declined from more than 1,009,000 in the census of 1910 to 658,220 in 1940. By 1960, there were only an estimated 321,774 speakers of Norwegian left, of whom 140,774 were first-generation Americans, whereas 141,000 were assumed to belong to the second and 40,000 to the third generation.[3] The percentage of Norwegian services in the Norwegian Lutheran Church in America, the largest Norwegian religious body in the United States, dropped from 73.1 percent in 1917 to 6.4 percent in 1944.[4] The number of Scandinavian-American weekly newspapers decreased from ninety-four in 1910 to thirty-two in 1940 to fourteen in 1960.[5]

While Norwegian language retention displayed similarities to that of other northern European groups, Norwegians preserved their mother tongue to a slightly greater extent than Danes and Swedes did. In 1940, 66.7 percent of second-generation Norwegian-Americans in North Dakota (the state with the highest Norwegian language retention) were capable of speaking their ancestral language; the percentage was higher in rural and lower in urban areas. Second-generation Swedes never attained a language retention rate above 55.1 percent (Minnesota); Danes did not even surpass 45.3 percent (Iowa).[6] Part of this discrepancy can be ascribed to outside variables such as relative population density and the ratio of rural versus urban settlement distribution.

World War I and its aftermath ended the period of largely unrestricted European emigration to the United States. The number of American residents born in Norway peaked in 1910, when it reached 403,858. Ten years later, it had declined to 363,862, and the National Origins Act of 1924 allotted Norway a yearly immigrant quota of only 2377.[7] This development further undermined the attempts to establish a permanent Norwegian-American subculture. Without the constant influx of new immigrants, the assimilation process accelerated further.

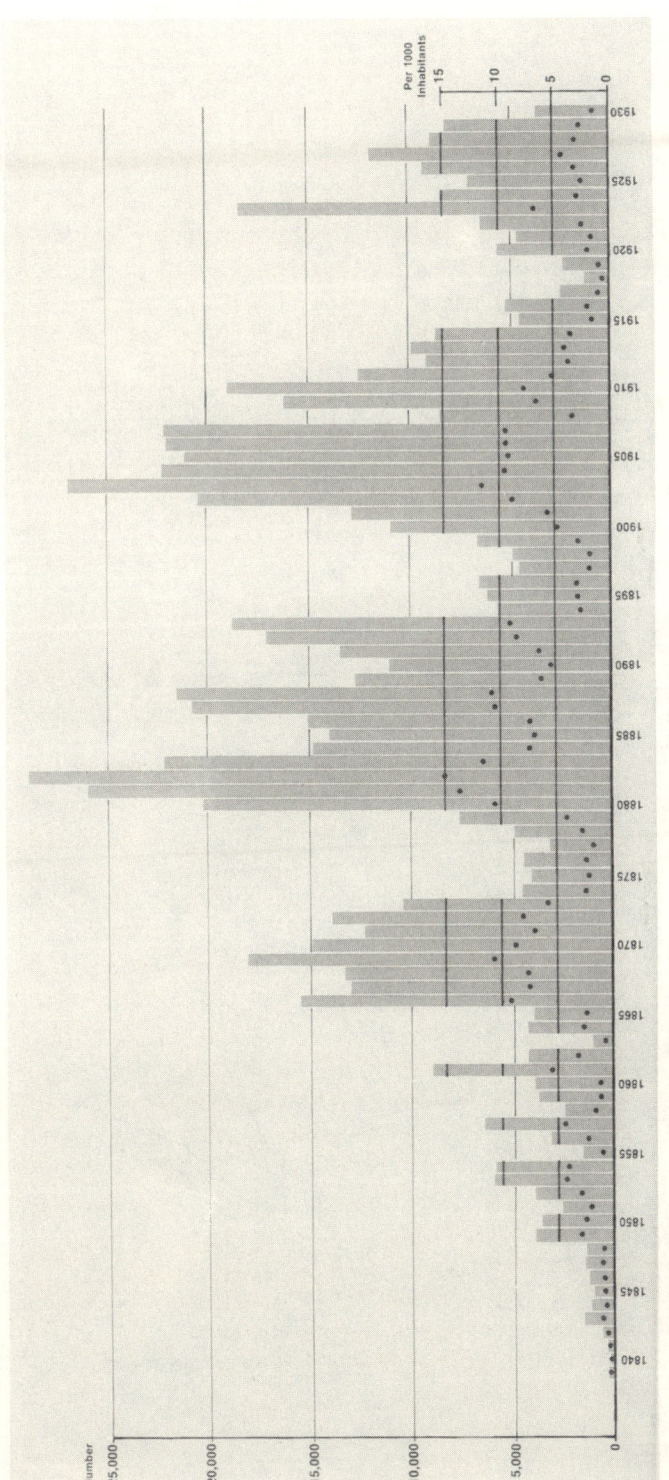

Norwegian emigration between 1840 and 1930. Source: Odd S. Lovoll, *The Promise of America: A History of the Norwegian-American People* (Minneapolis: University of Minnesota Press, 1984), 28. Copyright 1984 by Universitetsforlaget.

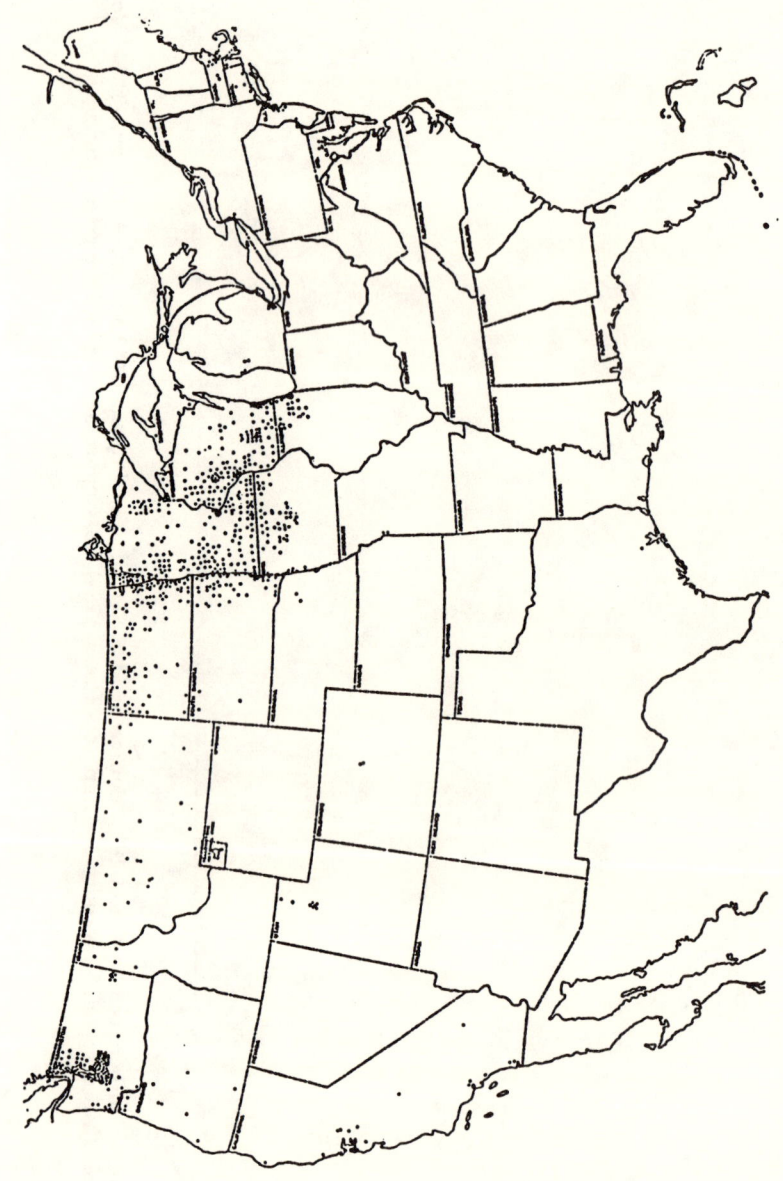

Norwegians in the United States, 1930
[Each dot represents a thousand Norwegian-born and native-born people of Norwegian parentage.] Source: Carlton C. Qualey, *Norwegian Settlement in the United States* (Northfield, Minn.: Norwegian-American Historical Society, 1938), 202–3.

Thus, the time period that witnessed the most noticeable public expression of the Norwegian presence in America also experienced its inner decline. The same apparent paradox manifests itself in the history of Norwegian-American literature, which bloomed in the first decades of the twentieth century and produced its most famous novels between World Wars I and II. A few years later, its time had virtually run out.

The understanding of the important role ethnicity has had and still has in the fabric of American society has grown considerably in recent scholarship. Ethnic literature is also political literature in the field of cultural politics; there exists a relationship between ethnic activism and ethnic literary production. It is, therefore, important to examine the strategies employed by ethnic writers in their attempt to convince their readership of their own cultural tenets. The political use of literature possesses relevance beyond the limits of ethnic authorship. The insights into the attitudes of Norwegian-American intellectuals toward their native culture and toward America that are gained from this investigation contribute, in turn, to an understanding of the attitudes displayed by more recent immigrant groups.

What are the constituent elements of an ethnic group? Usually, but not indispensably, ethnicity is directly connected with national origin. In the United States, ethnic groups provide a unit of reference and allegiance that is located between the levels of family and citizenship. As a rule, these groups are based on a communality of important identity markers such as culture, descent, or religion, frequently intertwined with one another. Religion can function both as a competitor with or as a constituent of ethnic identity. Social class will generally compete for allegiance with both religion and ethnicity, but economic division along ethnic lines can reinforce ethnic identity.

The history of European immigrant ethnicity in the New World to a large extent has been a history of acculturation and societal integration. Most attempts to preserve an encompassing separate cultural identity among participants in a voluntary, individually arranged migration had only limited success. Literary portrayals of the immigrant experience elaborate on its emotional side and promise to illuminate the psychology of cultural reorientation. In his study, *Assimilation in American Life,* which was near-paradigmatic for its era, Milton Gordon distinguished seven aspects of assimilation:

1. Cultural or behavioral assimilation, i.e., the change of cultural patterns to those of the host society.

2. Structural assimilation, i.e., large scale entry into institutions of the host society.
3. Marital assimilation, i.e., large scale intermarriage.
4. Identificational assimilation, i.e., a sense of peoplehood based exclusively on the host society.
5. Attitude receptional assimilation, i.e., the absence of prejudice against the immigrant.
6. Behavior receptional assimilation, i.e., the absence of discrimination against the immigrant.
7. Civic assimilation, i.e., the absence of value and power conflict.[8]

A look at present conditions illuminates how far the assimilation process has progressed in large segments of the Norwegian-American community with respect to Gordon's criteria; point four could arguably be an exception because of a continuous, if largely symbolic, allegiance to Norwegian peoplehood among some Norwegian-Americans.[9] Was this development inevitable? The fact that leading Norwegian-American intellectuals actively worked against it indicates, at the very least, that not everyone welcomed the process. The motivation for their resistance to Americanization is a significant topic of investigation in the present study.

The theoretical discussion has progressed since Gordon developed his theory of immigrant integration, and current scholarship largely rejects the proposition of an invariable linear development from original ethnicity to a projected Anglo-American conformity. The concept of a straight-line process of assimilation that inevitably turns European immigrants into indistinguishable members of Anglo-American society is no longer seen as a convincing reflection of a more complex reality.

The origin and content of ethnic identity in America has found a multitude of explanations. Following the terminology introduced by Edward Shils and Clifford Geertz, one school of thought explains ethnicity as an expression of primordial attachments. In his study, *Idols of the Tribe*, Harold Isaacs developed a comprehensive framework for this approach.[10] Ethnic identity is seen as a basic group identity into which every individual is born. Depending on the family, place, and time of his or her birth, the newborn shares a set of identification markers that will come to dominate his or her future identity. These markers include physical appearance, birthplace, name, language, history, religion, and nationality, all of which will normally be influenced, if not determined, by circumstances beyond the control of the individual. At the same time, an individual's sense of belonging will grow out of these primordial markers. Isaacs argues that humans judge social interactions in terms of a we-they dichotomy. In his work, *The Ethnic Phenomenon,* Pierre van den Berghe perceives this distinction between in-group and out-group as an outgrowth of kinship sentiments—ethnicity reflects a general human tendency toward nepotist behavior.

Other researchers have seen ethnicity as constructed more than inherited. Nathan Glazer and Daniel P. Moynihan used their experiences with New York city politics to define ethnicity as a strategy employed in the competition for scarce resources.[11] The literary scholar Werner Sollors, for his part, followed the constructed aspect of ethnic identity back to what he terms the invention of ethnicity.[12] Sollors sees ethnicity as a reaction of immigrant populations to the conditions in the new country. Ethnic life is reflected in symbols and metaphors; it is a symbolic construct that developed as a surrogate for the traditional loyalties that were lost under the impact of the modernization process. In the case of American immigrants, the cultural discontinuity to which they have all been subjected has only amplified this loss of tradition.

In their manifesto, "The Invention of Ethnicity: A Perspective from the U.S.A.," leading American immigration scholars from Kathleen Neils Conzen to Rudolph Vecoli present their cooperative conceptualization of ethnicity. They share the constructionist viewpoint forwarded by Sollors but insist on the necessity of fundamental prerequisites for this construction. The actual formulation of ethnic identity might be constructed as an adaptation to current conditions, but this construction did not occur in a vacuum; it relied on preexisting cultural, social, and historical experiences.

Conzen and her coauthors stress the importance of the immigrants themselves in defining their ethnicity. In a constant negotiation process, both within the group and vis-à-vis the majority population as well as other cultural communities, American ethnic groups form and develop their own identity. In their insistence on immigrant agency, the authors want to move away from a concept that focuses on individual immigrants, who are transformed by the majority culture exclusively on the latter's terms. Instead, they view American culture and identity as the result of ongoing encounters between different groups, in the course of which these groups managed to alter the concept of "American" to include aspects of their own background.

The increasing visibility of ethnic pride among societally integrated and acculturated European-Americans has found an alternative interpretation as well. Led by Herbert Gans, a school of immigration scholars has coined the term "symbolic ethnicity" to describe this phenomenon. Gans rejects the notion that a true revival of ethnicity among third- or fourth-generation European-Americans has taken place.[13] He concedes a renewed interest in ethnic self-identification and the embrace of visible symbols of a particular ethnic culture. He does not accept this development as the expression of an actual reintroduction of immigrant ethnicity, however.

Gans maintains that the average member of an American ethnic group is less interested in substantive participation in ethnic life—be it cultural or organizational—than in the preservation of an ethnic identity in a psychological sense. This identity is seen as purely self-chosen and voluntary; it is assumed by some and rejected by others. It is not a new phenomenon, but used to form an intrinsic component of a more comprehensive expression of ethnicity. While this psychological attachment was taken for granted by previous generations, it remains as a rather isolated symbolic allegiance in the more assimilated generations of today.

In spite of their sometimes antithetic scholarly presentation, these theories need not be seen as being as much in contrast to each other as has been conceived. The interplay between primordial theories that interpret ethnicity as the fulfillment of a general human desire for "belonging," theories that classify ethnic communities as interest groups mobilized to further their members' socioeconomic position, and theories that view ethnicity as constantly reconstructing itself around invented cultural symbols contribute to a more multifaceted explanation of the concept. Ethnic groups use their communal bonds in the service of their members and rely on handed down, created, or recreated symbols to strengthen their position both internally and vis-à-vis the majority population. In the course of European acculturation to America, some aspects of immigrant ethnic identity have remained more resilient than others, and the volatility of American identity has even led to attempts, however symbolic, at rediscovering a faded identity. In this study, ethnicity in the United States is viewed as the expression of an origin-oriented group identity characterized by the specific parameters present in an immigrant society.

Institutionalized Norwegian ethnicity in North America has displayed many facets. Hundreds of thousands eventually joined Norwegian churches. Most, but not all of them, were Lutheran, and in 1917 the merger of previously rival religious bodies led to the founding of the Norwegian Lutheran Church in America with nearly half a million members in more than three thousand congregations.[14] The Norwegian aspect had brought the different synods together but was nonetheless controversial from the beginning. It took the opponents of an ethnic Church almost thirty years to remove the word *Norwegian* from the Church's name, but when the change occurred in 1946, the synod had long ceased to be Norwegian in anything but name and tradition. In the subsequent decades, Lutheran Churches of various ethnic backgrounds have merged, further obscuring their original ethnic heritage. The increasing diversification of the American population has even resulted in conscious efforts to diminish the traditional preponderance of northern Europeans in the now completely Americanized Lutheran Church by establishing minority recruitment goals.

The Church also stood behind most attempts to establish Norwegian primary education in the new country. However, Norwegian-Lutheran parochial schools could not compete with the American common school for very long, and Norwegian instruction became restricted to summer school and confirmation class. The Norwegian language served largely as a means of access to Norwegian devotional literature in these institutions, and the switch to English occurred even faster in youth education than in regular congregational life. During the first decades of the twentieth century, Norwegian activists managed to introduce their native language as a subject to be taught in a number of Midwestern public schools, but the antiforeign agitation during and after World War I widely caused the termination of this practice.

For decades, Norwegian immigrants were able to follow events in the world—and particularly in their community—in their own press. The three biggest newspapers were *Skandinaven* (1866–1941), *Decorah-Posten* (1874–1972), and *Minneapolis Tidende* (1887–1935). At their peak, these papers had 54,000, 45,000, and 33,000 subscribers respectively.[15] In addition to these large, nationally distributed newspapers, there were many smaller, regional ones. The historic life cycle of the immigrant press parallels that of imaginative literature; only *Decorah-Posten*, as the inheritor of the other papers' surviving readers, managed to hold out longer.

Norwegian activities were not restricted to these primary undertakings. Based on immigrants' devotion to their Norwegian home districts, the *bygdelag* (village society) movement blossomed in the early twentieth century. Theaters, choirs, and sport clubs entertained the community. In the long run, however, only scholarly enterprises, such as the Norwegian-American Historical Association, or ethnic heritage associations directed at widely assimilated Norwegian-Americans with emotional ties to their ancestral homeland—most prominently the Sons of Norway—remained as the representatives of the formerly widespread Norwegian-American associational structure.

* * *

This study explores how Norwegian immigrant intellectuals in the United States used literature in the struggle to preserve a distinct Norwegian-American ethnic identity. Investigation of the connection between the authors' cultural ideology and the ideas forwarded by them in literary works demonstrates that immigrant authors frequently were also ethnic activists. The study is based on a specifically developed analytical approach that takes this fact into account while still distilling historically valuable information from immigrant literature. The concept of ethnicity is analyzed in the historical and political context of the immigrant experience; the analysis includes an examination of the social environment of both the Norwegian immigrant population in general and the immigrant author specifically.

The approach to ethnic literature differs in some important ways from the approach to literature in general.[16] While it is possible to examine a specific writer of immigrant background with traditional methods of textual analysis, the interest in and the significance of the writer will frequently be based less on formal masterfulness—if one accepts this elusive concept to begin with—than on the information about the immigrant experience contained in his or her works. Thus, even authors who might be regarded as mediocre according to an aesthetic canon can improve our understanding of the immigrants' living conditions and state of belonging at a specific point in time. Supported by a sociological examination of readership and dissemination, this idea-based approach promises more relevant results than a merely textual analysis.

There have also been attempts to read immigrant literature as historical writings; literary sources replaced missing historical evidence. It is important to remember that historical writing, and fiction to an even greater extent, is influenced by personal views. Historiography itself has come under attack for its purported speculativeness and lack of scientific rigor. While recognizing the subjective aspects present in all historical writing, this author still objects to surrendering the distinction between historical evidence and the literary portrayal of historical events. History as a discipline borders on the social sciences on the one side and on imaginative literature on the other. It distinguishes itself from fictional literature by its obligation to *strive* for truthful representation and to adhere to methodologies that support this proposition, and from the social sciences by not asserting to be capable of making human behavior predictable and explicable by systematic laws. The attempts of sociologists and political scientists to subsume social phenomena under general laws have always been open to question because they seem to level human differences and individualities. The increasing understanding of the relativity present even in the natural sciences has further questioned the ability of the social sciences to predict the outcome of the much more volatile phenomena they are describing.

Although history, as indicated, should not be equated with imaginative literature, historical writing can profit from the strength of its narrative. Hayden White and others have drawn attention to the role of fictional techniques in historiography.[17] Thus, one can see a continuum ranging from historical evidence via the narrative interpretation of such evidence to imaginative literature inspired by such evidence. This continuum demystifies the distinctions between different styles of history-based discourse, but it does not justify the reversal of its logical direction: it still does not permit treating historical fiction as primary historical evidence per se.

The limits imposed on the factual reliability of ethnic literature do not preclude its role as a source of historical information, as long as one remains aware of the literary quality of the works and their foundation in a cultural ideology—specifically, in the case of the authors examined in this study, that of cultural preservationism. These ideological influences constitute a worthwhile topic of investigation. Even more than authors in general, immigrant writers were part of the political and cultural debate within their communities. The overriding issue faced by them and the whole ethnic group was the survival of their distinct identity. Much of immigrant literature, almost by definition, revolves around the description of an identity different from that of the majority population. The end of this literature, on the other hand, is reached when the immigrants have disappeared into the dominant culture and population. In order to fully understand these works, one has to examine their underlying ideology and its literary expression.

Norwegian-American literature has not always been analyzed from an ethnic perspective. Traditionally, researchers examined individual works or authors, and while they did not ignore the ethnic aspect, they did not focus on it and rarely developed an overall insight into the specific qualities of ethnic literature. Dorothy Burton Skårdal introduced a new approach to the scholarship in the field with her book, *The Divided Heart*, in which she used the works of Scandinavian-American authors as historical source material. Disregarding the individual texts as literary entities, she extracted information on a multitude of historical and cultural aspects of the immigrant experience by comparing the various descriptions and drawing historical conclusions.

Most other researchers of ethnic literature stayed within the textual framework of individual works. Their works, as those of many other authors listed in the bibliography, are only briefly referred to in this study. By summarizing and interpreting a large number of texts, they presented an overall view of the specific literature. Allen Guttmann uses this approach in his book on Jewish authors, *The Jewish Writer in America*, as does Marcus Klein in his study of various groups, *Foreigners: The Making of American Literature, 1900–1940*. Neither these studies nor the eminent works on ethnicity that have accompanied the renewed interest in ethnic identity in the United States (by Nathan Glazer and Daniel P. Moynihan, Joshua Fishman, and Michael Novak, to name a few) have focused primarily on the relationship between literature and ethnicity.

Recently, Werner Sollors in *Beyond Ethnicity* and William Boelhower in *Through a Glass Darkly* have tried to develop a theoretical framework for the analysis of ethnic literature. Since ethnic literature depends on the survival of group identity, the relationship between the two deserves further examination, as does the role of the immigrant authors and their personal interests.

While it does not fall within the scope of this study to establish general parameters for the genre "ethnic literature," a few remarks about the ongoing debate seem appropriate. The examination of ethnicity and ethnic literature has received its impulses largely from an observation of immigrant societies, most often the United States. The American experience, which at least for Europeans largely expressed itself in a gradual acculturation that transformed immigrant subgroups into accepted members of American society within a few generations, leaves much room for disparate views on the exact point in time at which the passage to an exclusively American identity occurs. This problem is mirrored in the classification of literature as ethnic. Is immigrant literature defined by the use of a minority language? Or is it determined by its subject matter, i.e., immigrant literature is literature dealing with the immigrant experience? Dorothy Burton Skårdal represents a widely held view when she argues that texts about the personal experiences by first- and second-generation Americans are to be classified as ethnic literature, no matter which language they are in, whereas American literature in English that does not betray the writer's immigrant experience falls outside the scope of this genre.[18] She uses Carl Sandburg, who was of Swedish descent, to exemplify this boundary, classifying him as purely American.

William Boelhower argues that a separate investigation of ethnic literature contributes to its marginalization and views the terms *ethnic* and *American* as part of a single relational structure. His very theoretical reflections center on the concept of a cultural encyclopedia that guides the ethnic subject and describe ethnic semiotics as the interpretation of the genealogical history produced by the ethnic perspective. In a postmodern interpretation of ethnic semiosis he concludes that "far from being confined to the ethnic encyclopedia as a set of fixed cultural contents to be continually reproposed with each new generation, the ethnic subject now plays freely with the encyclopedia in order to produce an ethno-critical interpretation of the present and of the possibilities in it."[19] In simpler terms, Boelhower is arguing that cultural traditions should not be seen as static patterns merely to be followed, but as tools used to create new cultural expressions.

Werner Sollors analyzes the ethnicity of symbols and metaphors as well as of rites and rituals in American writing, demonstrating a particular interest in the connection between ethnicity and literary form. He accuses traditional critics of ethnic literature of being more interested in antiquarian questions along the lines of "How Portuguese is Dos Passos?" than in the exploration of the innovative aspects of this literature. He refers to Sandburg in his refutation of Skårdal, and his definition of ethnic literature manifests his primary concern: he defines it as "works written by, about, or for persons who perceived themselves, or were perceived by others, as members of ethnic groups, including even nationally and internationally popular writings by 'major' authors and formally intricate and modernist texts."[20] Sollors wants to free ethnic literature from the aura of parochialism by stressing its modernist aspects.

Both restrictive and comprehensive definitions of ethnic literature lead to practical difficulties. By excluding renowned authors of immigrant background whose writings do not concern themselves with their personal ethnicity, ethnic literature becomes parochial almost by definition. Widening the concept to include every writer who displays any form of immigrant background renders the category of ethnic literature virtually meaningless in a nation of immigrants such as the United States, because it would reclassify the bulk of American literature as "ethnic." This quantitative success would simultaneously deprive the concept of its practical value. If American literature is ethnic in its entirety, the particular quality of writers outside the English-speaking mainstream disappears.

The problem of classification partially manifests itself as an outgrowth of ethnic rivalry and the need for cultural assertion. If ethnic groups desire to flaunt renowned authors as their own, the question of a writer's ethnic belonging becomes politicized. Ethnic communities employ literary greats in their cultural mobilization against other communities, particularly against the majority population. The Anglo-American mainstream, for its part, has marginalized non-English expression in the United States by designating ethnic cultures as retrospective vestiges of obsolete foreign allegiances, devoid of any future perspective. Without this political instrumentalization, the specific quality of literature conceived at cultural crossroads could more easily receive an appropriate investigation, because the focus would no longer rest on the respective literary prowess of majority and minority culture. As soon as literary analysis no longer serves the purpose of evaluating the contribution of various subgroups to the national literary canon, the issue of classification will lose much of its emotional fervor.

After the arrival of the first Norwegian emigrant ship, the *Restauration,* in 1825, almost five decades had to pass until the Norwegian-American community was sufficiently established in the new country to produce an autonomous literature. Throughout its not very long history, this literature was created by people who devoted their spare time to their literary passion. Only one writer, the prolific and sensational Lars A. Stenholt, was able to earn a living by writing. The other authors not only suffered from their isolated location and their often limited formal education, but also from the time restraints put on them by their ordinary jobs. Waldemar Ager used the evening hours for his literary endeavors, whereas O. E. Rølvaag, as a professor at St. Olaf College, at least enjoyed the opportunity of an occasional sabbatical leave. The artistic isolation Norwegian-American authors found themselves in is reflected in a comment by the American writer Lincoln Colcord, who supplied the English translation of *Giants in the Earth.* After his initial consultations with Rølvaag, who as a college teacher had more access to the literary establishment than many other Norwegian-American writers, he marveled over Rølvaag's complete lack of connections to the American world of letters.[21] Most immigrant authors lived and produced secluded from the contemporary literary scene of both their homeland and their adopted country.

Dorothy Burton Skårdal quotes Simon Johnson's description of the conditions under which literature was produced:

> I know one who in stolen hours, preferably when bad weather hindered work outdoors, sat in a cold room and with numb fingers scrawled stories and poems about his people in this land. I know one who the whole day long—and it was not a mere eight-hour day either—followed his plow and harrow and composed verses which he tried to memorize until in a pause for rest he could scribble them down on a piece of wrapping paper....[22]

The first Norwegian literary texts in the United States scarcely concerned themselves with the ethnic question. The university professors Hjalmar Hjorth Boyesen and Rasmus B. Anderson published works with a European Scandinavian or historical background, such as Boyesen's *Gunnar* and Anderson's *America Not Discovered by Columbus*, whereas Nicolai Severin Hassel described dramatic events in the New World in his novel *Rædselsdagene, et norsk billede fra indianerkrigen* (The Days of Terror: A Norwegian Picture from the Indian War).[23] Many of the Norwegian-American institutions in whose defense preservationist authors were to rise in later decades had not even been established in the 1870s. Only when the immigrants had mastered the hardships of the settlement period did their numerical and financial strength begin to reflect itself in the creation of cultural institutions. It might seem ironic that by the beginning of the twentieth century, when an impressive network of newspapers, theaters, publishing houses, churches, language programs, and social institutions had been established, the underlying support for these institutions had already begun to erode. The number of first-generation Norwegian-Americans—and they were the people whose sacrifices had made these efforts possible—was gradually surpassed by that of American-born generations, who felt no deep practical need for them. The latter frequently viewed these institutions as luxuries and were indifferent or even hostile toward them. The American experience for most European immigrant groups has been that only the first generation depended on intra-ethnic organizations, whereas subsequent generations did not need intermediaries in their dealings with the majority society.

This change in attitude alarmed those writers who supported the continuation of a distinct Norwegian-American cultural realm. In spite of their frequent use of practical arguments, they were not primarily concerned with the pragmatic necessity of Norwegian cultural expression. They wanted to create a feeling of need within their community, because to them their national heritage represented a value in its own right. They were taken aback by the thought of completely forsaking their ancestral traditions, of being melted into a new entity. At the same time they, too, were witness to the power of assimilatory influences and did not themselves manage to escape them. The Norwegian-American Historical Association, founded in 1925 with the active participation of O. E. Rølvaag, found it necessary to conduct its business in English in order to attract competent scholars and to be certain that its message reached the younger generation. Waldemar Ager objected to this Anglicization, but not even he was able to raise all his children as Norwegian speakers. Preservationist authors might succeed in imparting to their children an active interest in matters Norwegian, but they could not prevent their socialization into the American mainstream.

Who were the people writing literature in their native language in a foreign land? Göran Stockenström investigated this question with regard to Swedish-Americans, and his findings will be largely applicable to the Norwegian community. Among slightly more than 200 writers, Stockenström found 132 journalists, 62 ministers, and 14 teachers or scholars.[24] Of the four Norwegian authors whose works will be examined in this study, two were journalists, one a scholar, and one a farmer who regularly contributed to newspapers.

The Swedish historian Harald Runblom classifies (Scandinavian) immigrant authors according to six categories:

1. Authors both writing in the homeland language and publishing in the homeland but having experience as immigrants in America.
2. Authors writing in the homeland language, starting their careers as writers in the homeland but completing them as immigrants in America.
3. Authors writing in the homeland language but with their careers wholly in America.
4. Immigrant authors publishing in the homeland language and in English with their careers in America.

5. Authors writing almost wholly in English, aiming at a public outside their own immigrant group and with a literary production that reflects their immigrant background.
6. Immigrant authors writing in English who have adapted to American style and motives.[25]

Runblom puts O. E. Rølvaag into category four, probably correctly so, even though the preponderance of his Norwegian writing would also warrant a place in category three, with the other authors examined in this study. Although one can question the overall value of this detailed categorization of a continuum, it does, at the very least, draw attention to the considerable diversity within immigrant literature.

The novels selected for this study, Waldemar Ager's *Paa veien til smeltepotten* (On the Way to the Melting Pot, 1917), Simon Johnson's *Frihetens hjem* (Freedom's Home, 1925), Hans Rønnevik's *100 procent* (100 Percent, 1926), and Ole Edvart Rølvaag's *Peder Seier* (Peder Victory, 1928) and *Den signede dag* (The Blessed Day, 1931; the English translations of these books were titled *Peder Victorious* and *Their Fathers' God*) appeared during the period that began with America's entry into World War I. Within less than two decades, the cultural and particularly the linguistic demise of Norwegian-America became manifest; the novels were chosen because of their opposition to this process. Rølvaag, Ager, and Johnson generally are counted among the four great figures of Norwegian-American literature—selecting them seemed self-evident. Johannes Wist is looked upon as the fourth leading author, but he cannot be considered a true preservationist because he never believed in the viability of a permanent Norwegian-American subculture. Hans Rønnevik, on the other hand, shares many basic beliefs with the other three, and his novel displays similarities with Simon Johnson's *Frihetens hjem*. Both examine the atmosphere during World War I and revolve around a preservationist protagonist who is forced to justify his views in court. The outcomes of this experience differ widely, opening valuable opportunities for comparison. *100 procent* also measures up to *Frihetens hjem* artistically; the author deservedly received The Norwegian Society of America's literary prize for the novel.[26] The interest in the preservation of Norwegian life in America shared by these writers is reflected in their literary works; therefore, an examination of these works provides information on the purpose and the impact of both this and other types of activist literature.

Significantly, all four authors spent large parts of their lives in the

Upper Midwestern core territory of Norwegian settlement, and all the novels examined are situated there. The area encompassed by Eau Claire, Wisconsin (Ager); Fargo, North Dakota (Johnson); Northfield, Minnesota; and Canton, South Dakota (Rølvaag) corresponds to a high degree to the heartland of Norwegian-America. In this central cultural landscape, the idea of establishing a permanent Norwegian-American subculture seemed feasible; in general, only intellectuals who experienced the blossoming of Norwegian ethnicity on the prairie fully mustered the energy and the inspiration necessary for immigrant preservationism.

* * *

All the works selected center on the question of ethnic identity. Since previous scholarship has not yet presented fully satisfying analytical tools for such texts, this study proposes and uses its own, specifically developed methodological approach, which should become a useful instrument for all analysts of activist literature. Through the juxtaposition of belletristic and nonbelletristic discourse, the ideas expressed in the literary works examined are compared to the arguments the authors put forward in their nonfiction writings. The rendition of the plot is reduced to its ethno-ideological nucleus and followed by an examination of the authors' rhetorical strategies. It is supplemented by an analysis of the texts' reception and their influence in the target readership. Finally, the various styles are contrasted with regard to their ideological message and its artistic realization.

This leads to the following compact definition of the methodology: *The ethnic component contained in the texts is examined at the intersection between narrative sequence and condensed ideological topicality against the background of community reception and politicized ethnicity.* Such an analysis should provide the optimal results for this specific literary category and can be further clarified by a graphic representation.

The graph on the opposite page visualizes how the crisscross analysis of issues and plot allows a more accurate determination of the cultural ideology. Building on the investigation of the community reception and of the larger intellectual environment in which this literature took shape—represented by the two concentric circles—the condensed plot rendition (horizontal arrow) intersects with issue extraction (vertical arrow) to form a tight interpretative web.

As part of the analysis of the Norwegian-American situation, comparisons with other ethnic groups place the findings into a broader

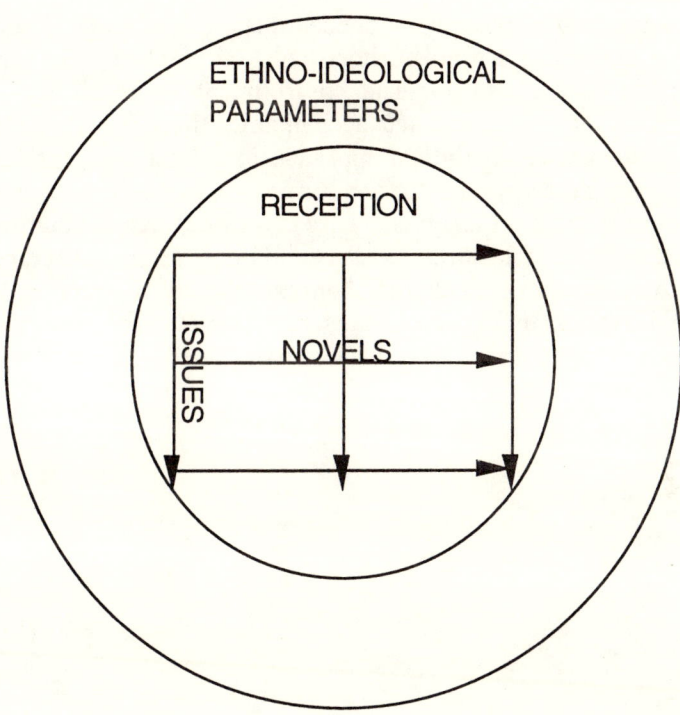

context and integrate abstract, non-group-specific social mechanisms. An intimate knowledge of more than one ethnic community contributes decisively to the recognition of underlying patterns in immigrant behavior and can prevent undue generalizations. This study draws on the experiences of German-Americans, whose cultural and regional affinities make them comparable to the Norwegians, whereas their greater numbers increased their visibility in the eyes of the Anglo-American majority and exacerbated majority reaction toward them. This combination of differences and similarities allows the most instructive general comparisons, whereas the similarities of the Swedish-American experience can at times supplement the Norwegian source material.

A material aspect of the study lies in its intent to create a methodological means for the examination of ethnic and/or activist literature. It does not deliver new text-based interpretations of the literary works selected; its purpose is not to provide an alternative reading of previously analyzed works of art. Nor does it follow the antipodal approach of treating literature as primary source material for the social conditions it describes. These texts refer to sociohistoric conditions, but they are not used as primary evidence for these conditions. They serve as source material for their authors' cultural ideology, whereas their relationship to their sociological environment is established by the analysis and interpretation that accompanies them.[27]

The study's novel analytical approach integrates perspectives from several scholarly disciplines for the purpose of extracting socially relevant information from imaginative texts without overestimating their potential as historical source material.[28] By putting these literary writings into their wider ideological context, the study searches for the kind of historical information they *can* provide: the worldview of Norwegian-American activist intellectuals.

2
Assailing the Melting Pot—Waldemar Ager

WALDEMAR AGER WAS BORN IN 1869 IN THE SOUTHEAST NORWEGIAN town of Fredrikstad. His father moved to Chicago in 1883 to establish a tailor shop; the family followed two years later. Waldemar began to work as an apprentice printer for a Norwegian-American newspaper and soon joined an abstinence society, therewith identifying early on with his two lifelong political concerns: Norwegian cultural preservation and the temperance movement. In 1892, after a short stay in Milwaukee, he moved to Eau Claire, which remained his home for the rest of his life. He worked as a printer for the Norwegian temperance weekly *Reform*, assuming its coeditorship in 1896 and its sole editorship in 1903. *Reform* and Waldemar Ager became synonyms. In 1905, Ager also started the quarterly *Kvartalskrift* (Quarterly), published for The Norwegian Society of America, a Norwegian cultural organization. He served as the editor of this journal until its discontinuation in 1922.

Waldemar Ager did not restrict his writing to journalism but also embarked on a literary career, which began in 1894 with *Paa drikkeondets konto: Fortællinger og vers* (Charged to the Account of the Evils of Drinking: Short Stories and Verse). His fiction, like his journalism, is deeply influenced by his political convictions: Ager was very active in temperance societies and in Norwegian-American organizations and even ran for office on the ticket of the Prohibition party.[1] His struggle for abstinence and cultural preservation increasingly isolated him during his final years, by which time many of his brothers-in-arms had deserted him. Waldemar Ager died in 1941.

Paa veien til smeltepotten (On the Way to the Melting Pot), published in 1917, cannot be understood without considering its origin in the heated atmosphere of World War I. America's participation in the war was accompanied by an intense propagandistic effort, directed first against Germany, then against German-Americans, and finally against non-British immigrants in general. Laws were passed against the use of "foreign" languages in schools and churches; some places even prohibited their use in the streets and over the telephone.[2] The drive toward assimilation intensified and cast suspicion on everything written in a language other than English. In his novel, Ager fought back by illustrating the negative aspects of assimilation to his fellow Norwegian-Americans.

* * *

Paa veien til smeltepotten opens with the arrival of the young Norwegian Lars Olson in a Norwegian-American town. People live comfortably there. Members of the older generation have worked hard and achieved a high standard of living, which is enjoyed heartily by their American-born children. The latter largely depend on their family and show little interest in work; nevertheless, they are admired by their parents and by newcomers such as Lars for their more refined manners and their excellent command of the English language. The children, on the other hand, are embarrassed by their parents' foreignness.

From the beginning of the novel, the hierarchical relationship between Norwegian and Anglo-American is established. Mrs. Omley, the wife of a small Norwegian-American businessman, prepares a traditional New England dinner of the kind she has read about in an American newspaper for her mainly Norwegian guests because there will be one native-born American among them and because she wants to impress her fellow immigrants. At the party, the guests attempt to outdo each other by interjecting more or less appropriate English phrases into their Norwegian conversation. The two daughters, Mabel Overhus and Sophy Omley, who are put in charge of serving the food, address everyone in English. Mrs. Omley was upset about how difficult it was to enlist Sophy's help, but when Sophy answered her in fluent English and sulked just like an upper-class American girl, she is overwhelmed by her daughter's American gracefulness. The girls are perfectly capable of speaking Norwegian, as they prove when they want to converse with the young newcomer Lars Olson, who has arrived knowing little English. They would never use Norwegian in public, but in the privacy of the kitchen there is no reason to feel embarrassed.

One of the guests, Mrs. Stenson, never fails to impress her immigrant peers. As a nursemaid for an American family, she has picked up expressions that the other women can only listen to in silent admiration. All the Norwegians agree that they should emulate the Ameri-

Waldemar Ager.
Courtesy Norwegian-American Historical Association.

cans as thoroughly as possible, except for the husband of the only native-born American present.[3] He is merely a plumber, but he managed to realize the dream of many male immigrants: to marry an elegant American lady. As the only guest who believes in bilingual education for Norwegian-American children, he criticizes an educational system that teaches the children Latin or German, but not the language of their parents. They learn about the old Egyptians, but not about their own ancestors.

The pastor of the principal Norwegian-American congregation also attends the party. He is no friend of the Norwegian language and was chosen to replace his predecessor because the congregation wanted to add English services to the then exclusively Norwegian ones. His early experiences with the Norwegian language were marred by convoluted words like *retfærdiggjørelse* (absolution) and *vederstyggelighed* (abomination), which abounded in the catechism studied in the Norwegian religion school. The family spoke English at home, but his father insisted on his attending this school. At the seminary, he became almost fluent in Norwegian, but it always remained a foreign language to him.

The pastor expects that the church will eventually switch completely to English, but he hesitates to offend the older members of the congregation for fear of losing their much needed financial support. He wants to construct a new, modern church that will attract English-speakers. The plumber views this plan as another example of how the Norwegians are regarded as good enough to build something, only to be thrown out after the work is completed; they are even expected to "pay for the rope that will be used to hang them." He reminds the pastor and the other guests how hard the immigrants worked to establish their simple church, which is not good enough for their children now, but his Norwegian friends consider comparisons between the immigrants and their more refined Americanized children inappropriate.

A serious generation gap has developed in the immigrant community. Just as Mrs. Omley is in awe of her daughter, who is as elegant and assimilated in appearance as she is idle, her husband is enthralled with watching his boys spend their days playing ball in the American middle-class tradition of the best parts of town. Berntine Nelson, the widow with whom Lars Olson boards, marvels how a simple woman such as herself could have borne and raised a son as genteel as her Henry. The latter is actually not very brilliant off the football field, but his mother, who understands very little English, does not notice. She is proud to have a son who has never learned much Norwegian;

all the more so because it equally impresses her friends, all of whom are immigrant women like her. One of these friends, Mrs. Dale, likes to show off the English letters she receives from her daughter Gertie, who works for an American family in a neighboring town. The only thing that diminishes this maternal success in the eyes of the other immigrant women is everyone's recollection of Gertie speaking Norwegian as a little child and merely forgetting the language later in life. After proudly displaying the letters, Mrs. Dale has to find someone to translate them into Norwegian—the only language she can understand.

The younger Norwegian-Americans accept their parents' lack of American sophistication in exchange for being indulged by them—at least as long as the parents do not embarrass them in public. The children entertain visiting friends in the elegant living room and draw attention to their parents' stately portraits on the wall, but they avoid presenting father and mother in person. They grow up without exposure to their parents' background, and while they try to emulate American models, they lack access to the more sophisticated cultural patterns internalized in established Anglo-American family settings. They acquire the expectations and tastes of a lifestyle that is not their own. Whereas upper-class American children continue their schooling at college and the newcomers go to work at sixteen, first-generation Norwegian-Americans lack direction after graduating from high school. They do not have the means to attend college, but they regard manual labor as beneath them.

Lars is deeply impressed by his experiences in the new country. He writes to his friends and family in Norway and describes how he was invited to the home of his employer and met "important" people there—a situation that would never arise in the old country. He begins to dream about a refined American wife and starts to court Sophy Omley. She is not unreceptive, but her family dislikes the prospect of a newcomer as a son-in-law because they could have saved the money spent on Sophy's education had they known she would waste herself on an unsophisticated immigrant. They treat her with less respect and increase her domestic workload; after all, she will be a common man's wife. As a consequence, Sophy develops second thoughts about the marriage. When one of the young Omley boys expresses the family's general sentiments by throwing a snowball at Lars, Sophy's suitor feels humiliated by the unmistakable amusement of the Omleys and leaves in anger. At first he hopes that Sophy will ask him to return, but when she departs for college without contacting him, his thoughts revert to his old friend Karoline Huseby in Norway, and he invites her to join him. After a period of consideration, she accepts the invitation and sets out for America.

Karoline does not fall for the lure of quick success and assimilation. She surprises Lars by being able to speak English when she arrives, but to his dismay she remains noticeably Norwegian. Lars desires to transform her into an American lady; the failure of these attempts rekindles his aspirations to find a more refined wife, with whom he could impress people both at church and on social occasions. By founding a Good Templar lodge, the couple manage to revive the fond memories they share of a similar lodge in Norway. For a while this experience reinforces the bond between them, but Lars views the lodge predominantly from a business perspective and soon loses interest in it.

Karoline finds work as a servant girl at the house of Judge Highbee. The judge descends from an old New England family, and Karoline feels comfortable in the noble ambiance of his home. When the college-educated sons of the household cannot translate the inscription on a German beerstein, the Alsatian kitchen girl recognizes it as Latin, and the embarrassed Highbees realize that their servants know more Latin than they do. Karoline wears a Norwegian ribbon on that country's national holiday, whereupon she is criticized by one of the judge's guests, who is of Scandinavian immigrant background herself, for not appreciating the freedom America offers and displaying the colors of the repressive country she hails from. Karoline is not intimidated and retorts that she enjoyed as much freedom in Norway as she has in the United States, indeed more, because Norway, unlike the United States, grants women the right to vote. This response impresses the judge and the other guests, and all the women present cut off a little piece of Karoline's ribbon to wear in honor of Norway. Judge Highbee even orders that two American flags be hoisted to celebrate this occasion.

After the temporary specter of a simple Norwegian immigrant for a son-in-law, the Omley family is overjoyed when their daughter marries a young man who not only works as an assistant cashier at the local bank but is of Scottish descent. It soon turns out, however, that the newlyweds live beyond their means, and father Omley has to subsidize their lifestyle. In addition, he, like the other Norwegians, feels the need to improve his home, mainly because of the children, who cannot be expected to live in their parents' simple house. Whereas most of his fellow immigrants are satisfied with adding on to their existing homes, Omley builds a new mansion-type residence. The great costs of keeping up the new house, combined with the expenses of his children, disturb Omley's peace of mind. The middle-class American in him accepts the financial burden as part of the social standing he has achieved, whereas the Norwegian immigrant in him is appalled at the waste of money. When he is defrauded in an investment made upon the advice of his son-in-law and in conflict with his "Norwegian" inner self, the financial losses undermine his nerves and his health. On his deathbed, he speaks Norwegian to his youngest son, tells him all about his youth in Norway, and wants him to be confirmed in Norwegian so he will forget neither God nor his father. After the funeral, a journalist asks his adult children about their father's background and life, but they know nothing about him.

The store owner Thore Overhus is equally dissatisfied with his life and reminisces about the days when he and his wife were poor newcomers in Chicago. They did not have much money, but they followed their own path and they cared for each other. Now he feels that he has lost control over his environment; everything in his house is modeled after other people's tastes. His Norwegian mementos have been replaced with international and American pieces of the kind seen in Yankee homes. He no longer lives with *his* wife but with a bad copy of Cameron's or Smith's wife, and his children have become completely alien to him. If he speaks Norwegian at home, everyone is upset; if he uses English, everyone corrects him. His wife restricts her Norwegian to communication with Lars, in order to remind him of his status as a recent arrival. Overhus increasingly withdraws to the backstairs of his house or spends all his time at the store. Only after financial difficulties have driven him to suicide does his wife realize the emptiness of her ambitions and begin to retreat to the same backstairs that were her husband's final refuge.

The circumstances in the Skare family have always been particularly unpleasant. Mother Skare never learned much English, and the children do not know Norwegian. After the death of his first wife, Mr. Skare had gone to Norway to find a mother for this two daughters. The older children only spoke English and subsequently established English as the language for their younger siblings as well. When he is at home, the father serves as a translator; otherwise, the children communicate with their mother through signs and in a Skare house pidgin. Mrs. Skare works day and night for her uncooperative children, who see her as an irreplaceable part of the household, always at hand, but more an appliance than a human being. During her endless housework, Mrs. Skare talks to herself in Norwegian, reproving her children's behavior. Only Lars hears her—a mother who cannot have a sensible conversation with her own children, who has not been able to talk to them since they were small. Finally, her nerves crack. She believes that she has a flock of six-year-old children—a reference to the age at which they moved out of her cultural realm—and has to be committed to a mental hospital.

Mrs. Skare is not the only immigrant unable to cope with the pressures and mores of the new country. The Morstuens—their son has changed his name to Morestew—are an old Norwegian couple whose children have dispersed all over North America and who themselves never managed to establish a lasting home in the new country. Their retirement to town was meant to grant them peaceful final years, but Mrs. Morstuen is unnerved by voices that speak to her every night. She is convinced that Indians are after her to avenge the desecration of a burial ground, and she eventually passes on these hallucinations to her husband. These aging immigrants have achieved material success through their emigration, but money cannot alleviate their loneliness.

Problems of a different kind plague the younger generation. In their desire to rise socially, they distance themselves from their parents' class, but they are not accepted by the leaders of local society they aspire to join. That is why Mabel Overhus has not found a husband and why Mrs. Dale's daughter is left alone with an illegitimate child by the son of a leading Yankee family. Even Lars Olson, himself a newcomer, is in the grip of similar ambitions, and his relationship with Karoline suffers because of this. He wants to change jobs and hopes to combine a professional with a social ascent.

Lars's friend Henry Nelson has accomplished exactly that. After much initial resistance, Edith Perkins' wealthy father accepts Henry as his son-in-law. He decides to support him and even sends him to college, whereupon Mrs. Nelson, whose life revolves around her son's success, embarrasses the well-to-do Perkinses by handing them her hard-earned savings as a contribution to Henry's education. After graduation, Henry is put to work by Mr. Perkins, but his skills do not match his rank. He is of little value to the company and cannot find satisfaction in his undemanding employment. With his young wife, he takes his mother into their house to show her their gratitude, but Mrs. Nelson regards life in the elegant new surroundings as just another sacrifice made on behalf of her son. Nevertheless, she becomes upset when a friend implies that she could have related more easily to a normal working girl as a daughter-in-law, because she considers

Henry above such a marriage. Upon realizing that Henry is dissatisfied with his life and would prefer to move away, Mrs. Nelson makes a last sacrifice. Knowing that he would not leave as long as she is alive, she refuses to eat during an illness and dies.

Visiting Mrs. Nelson on her deathbed, the pastor has to practice his constantly deteriorating Norwegian. He knows from experience that the immigrants always return to their native language at the end. He cannot understand why English was good enough for them when they were healthy and strong but does not seem to suffice during their final hours. The pastor dreads these occasions because he senses that his words fail to console, and he is looking forward to the time when he will be able to fulfill his duties solely in English. When one of his sermons is based on the biblical story about Esau selling his birthright as the first-born son, he uses the analogy of the Norwegian immigrants who sell their Lutheran belief for material goods. Karoline considers this interpretation too narrow; it should include their complete heritage, not only their religion. Like many newcomers, she is drawn to a more modest church that uses Norwegian for all its activities.

As Lars tries to be as American as possible, he does not emulate the refined societal aristocracy represented by Judge Highbee; instead, he follows the example set by the ambitious, pushy frontier environment around him. He always "talks shop"; there is nothing more fascinating to him than conversation about his business activities. He has turned into a skillful salesman who preys on the psychological weaknesses of his customers. Among other things, he facetiously "admits" to the Norwegians that the local competition is successful with the immigrants but adds that the clientele for Overhus' more expensive store attracts the American segment of the population. Consequently, many Norwegians switch their business to Overhus. When Karoline finally accepts that Lars has become a stranger to her and terminates their engagement, the latter can realize his old dream. He marries Mabel Overhus, who has to salvage the family business after her father's suicide, and becomes co-owner of a store and proud husband of an elegant American lady at the same time.

Karoline returns to Norway, but she cannot forget America. Through her new job as a nurse, she meets a well-educated Norwegian physician with whom she discusses her American experiences. They both admire the nobility expressed by New England's leading families, who lack the arrogance of the Norwegian aristocracy. The doctor observes that both these Yankee aristocrats and the simple, devout immigrant pioneers are disappearing rapidly in the emerging materialistic culture. Although Karoline gradually reacclimates in Norway, where she will eventually live as the physician's wife, she takes one last trip to America. She notices how the Norwegians have continued their march toward spiritual poverty in the guise of material success, and her former fiancé exemplifies this process most dramatically. Karoline cannot recognize this hectic businessman, subservient and cunning at the same time, as the Lars Olson of her youth. He is ready for the big melting pot.

When Henry Nelson worked at an iron foundry, he encountered a real-life melting pot. Many different pieces of inferior scrap metal were being melted down, and Henry observed how only broken and otherwise useless material was used, never functioning machinery. The manager refused to melt down other people's machines, because he foresaw the time when his machines would end up in a junkyard. He designated the material he gained from scrap for the simplest parts of his new machines. With regard to humans, he did not trust people who tried to assimilate, preferring recent arrivals from Germany or Scandinavia for responsible positions at the foundry and people of his own Yankee stock for his private contacts.

Ager concludes his novel with the image of Norwegian immigrants getting ready for the melting pot. They have sacrificed what was dear to them: their love of family and religion, the songs and memories of their youth, and the traditions and the language of their native culture. They filled the emptiness these sacrifices produced with love for themselves and for material possessions. In order to hide from themselves and God, they change their names and appearance. Now they are marching toward their final destination: some with the joyful expectation of contributing to the creation of a brand-new metal, others unthinkingly following the path of least resistance. Lars has prepared himself well for the cauldron by shedding his best qualities first, because those pieces that have lost their own specific character, whose original purpose one no longer can tell, make the best raw material for the melting pot.

* * *

Paa veien til smeltepotten was one of Ager's most critical books, and some Norwegian-Americans felt that it did not do them justice. Finishing the novel in 1917 during the increasing war-time commotion, Ager foresaw the demise of Norwegian-America even before the legal and political pressures emanating from the mainstream institutions and populace further curtailed the chances for an autonomous

Norwegian future in America. In Ager's book, assimilation is not so much based on outside intervention, but on the character flaws of the immigrants themselves. In their quest for material success, they view their cultural identity as useless ballast and throw it overboard. They are in awe of their children, who effortlessly achieve the American identity that eludes them in spite of their efforts. These children, on the other hand, are used to the support and admiration of their hardworking family and harbor illusions about their true standing in society. They fail to realize that, to the American upper class, they are still the offspring of immigrant laborers.

Ager maintains that the people he sees as the real Americans, namely, the old-stock New England families, remain aloof from the materialistic culture and ethnic intermarriage. They preserve their own identity and leave the melting pot to the immigrants. They do not feel the need to disavow their knowledge of or interest in foreign languages and culture, as do the immigrants.

Does, however, the feeling of inferiority originate in the minds of the immigrants? In reality, the immigrants did not arrive in the new country feeling ashamed of their background; it was the reception in the host country that produced this inferiority complex. In Ager's novel the immigrants themselves stand behind the Americanization drive, but the local environment portrayed is rather unusual. The novel is set in a Midwestern town, but we notice little of the political and cultural influence of the dominant Yankee establishment. Ager even implies that the Americans would respect immigrants more if they preserved their own customs. Although cultural pluralists of this sort did exist among the American leaders of those days, they were undoubtedly in the minority. Realistically, most of the pressure to assimilate originated from American society at large; Ager puts too much blame on the shoulders of his fellow immigrants. The portrayal of immigrants who continue to read foreign newspapers, but hide this activity from the community, seems plausible, but this conduct is more likely in a social environment that differs from the one described in *Paa veien til smeltepotten*. Although immigrants could consider it necessary to hide their ethnic affiliation, they were less likely to do so in surroundings dominated by their own group than in an atmosphere in which they felt more isolated.

Similarly, it remains doubtful whether the children of the immigrants felt superior to their parents because of their parents' self-image. After all, they *were* better-versed in the language and in the mores of the new country; that the parents were regarded as outsiders by society at large was not contingent on their acknowledgment of this fact. Both parents and children merely reflected the values expressed by the American society in which they were living. If the question is reduced to an intergenerational, intrafamiliar one, the picture remains incomplete.

One of the features that leaves the most discomforting impression is expressed realistically in the intrafamiliar relationship, however. The fact that parents and children cannot communicate normally reveals a sometimes overlooked aspect of the immigrant experience. While communication as limited as in Ager's Skare family may have been unusual, most immigrant parents were faced with severe limitations when handing down family traditions and values if their children were not fluent in the ancestral tongue. An abundance of rituals and experiences, often related to the parents' own childhood and to their familiar customs, was untranslatable. Some of the materialism ascribed to American culture might trace back to this rupture in the intergenerational spiritual lifeline—to a loss of everyday cultural tradition that was caused not only by the worldwide forces of modernization, but also by the specific immigrant quality of the American experience.

The Church plays a smaller role in *Paa veien til smeltepotten* than in many comparable Norwegian-American novels. It does not serve as the moral backbone of the immigrant community and fails to form a bastion of Norwegian culture. The urban setting might explain this fact. A close look unveils the absence of any organized Norwegian ethnic activity in this town. If we discount Karoline's brief appearance and her activities in the temperance lodge, only the plumber expresses a preservationist perspective. The process of assimilation advances not only without pressure groups favoring it—as previously indicated—but also without any organized resistance. There is no reference to a bitter struggle about the future of the Norwegian language in church; only an expectation of a gradual but unstoppable displacement of Norwegian practices. At the same time, working people of both rural and urban background continue to use their native language, as exemplified by the road crew and the farm girls.

This lack of organized activity on either side of the language question contrasts with the picture presented in other descriptions—fictional or nonfictional—including the three other novels analyzed in this study. Is it necessarily incorrect, however? Is it not likely that a large percentage of the population was little touched by the intense political debate over these issues? Plausibly, much of this discussion took place among intellectuals, whereas average immigrants went about their daily lives and viewed the immigrant community from the perspective of its economic and psychological usefulness more than seeing it as a value in itself. The frustration Ager harbored over this noncommittal attitude clearly inspired the sarcasm that permeates the novel, because in the activist's world view, the ethnic community did possess abstract importance.

All the immigrants eventually failed—if not financially, then at least spiritually. This harsh verdict deserves closer scrutiny. Ager pointed out how empty the lives of these outwardly successful people had become, and he blamed their greed and their weakness of character for this emptiness. This leads to the question of whether they would really have been so dissatisfied with their lives if it was their shallowness that had brought them into this situation to begin with. In other words, if the immigrants were as materialistic and self-centered as Ager implied, why would they not have been satisfied with their empty but comfortable lifestyle? This logical difficulty forced Ager to introduce a series of financial disasters that undermined the material well-being of the leading immigrants. The fact that Ager's characters only discover the spiritual paucity of their lives when faced with economic misfortune might explain why Norwegian-Americans in real life failed to view their development as negatively as did Ager. Clearly, the author used artistic freedom in his creation of the immigrants' economic development, because the proportion of failed businesses in the novel is too high to reflect Norwegian-American reality. The author's perceived need to exaggerate the economic adversities in order to make his point convincingly to his intended audience indicates the overriding importance that the immigrants attached to their financial situation.

In his dramatic personalization of the melting pot concept, Ager sums up his ideological message. Only the worst traits will survive the melting process, and the final product will be of little value to the new country. The immigrants are divesting themselves of their finest emotions in their vain hope to ascend to new heights, following an idea that the leaders of the nation only consider appropriate for the masses, not for themselves. This melting pot, for which he uses the Norwegian-English hybrid word *smeltepotten*, looms as the destiny Ager wanted to warn his fellow Norwegian-Americans about. Like other cultural preservationists, he was convinced that Norwegian immigrants could make a more valuable contribution to America's development if they remained true to themselves and to their heritage.

3
Simon Johnson: A Chronicler of His Time

SIMON JOHNSON WAS BORN IN THE SMALL GUDBRANDSDAL TOWN OF Øyer in 1874; the Gudbrandsdal is Norway's central valley and an area with a rich folk culture. When Johnson was eight, his family settled in North Dakota, where he attended the American public school during the regular school year and the Norwegian parochial school in the summer. In 1910, he embarked on a one-year journey to Norway to rediscover his heritage. Ten years later, he assumed the editorship of the Norwegian-American paper *Normanden* in Grand Forks, and in 1929 he accepted a position on the editorial board of the respected *Decorah-Posten,* where he worked until his retirement in 1945.

Simon Johnson was one of the leading figures on the Norwegian-American literary scene and received the literary prize of The Norwegian Society of America. He published six major literary works during the time period spanning from *Et geni* (A Genius) in 1907 to *Frihetens hjem* (Freedom's Home) in 1925 and contributed to various publications until his death in 1970.

Frihetens hjem was published in 1925 as the sequel to *Fallitten paa Braastad* (Bankruptcy at Braastad), which had appeared three years earlier. The two novels provide a fictional account of the experiences of the Braastad family on the North Dakota prairie. Jens Braastad and his wife Lisa left their Norwegian homeland because they saw no chance for economic betterment there. The Braastads were *husmenn* (cotters), and in the rigid Norwegian class system, proprietorship seemed an unattainable dream. The Braastads therefore embarked on the journey to North America, as did so many of their countrymen. Jens Braastad was a strong and hardworking man and eventually became the richest and most powerful farmer in his area.

The novels do not restrict themselves to narrating the story of the Braastad clan, however. If this were the case, they might not deserve to be the topic of a study today. Their artistic merits have not been

Simon Johnson.
Courtesy Norwegian-American Historical Association.

able to impart to them a place among the literary classics, and interest in the personal experiences of the Braastads has decreased over the years. What makes *Frihetens hjem,* in particular, so valuable is its position right at the center of the debate about the future of Norwegian ethnicity in the United States. The novel's political character provides us with an opportunity to examine the arguments used by the generation that tried to maintain a distinct Norwegian-American culture. *Fallitten paa Braastad,* the first part of the story, does not discuss this subject matter and therefore only will provide such information as is necessary for the understanding of subsequent events.

* * *

Jens Braastad has become the wealthiest farmer in the settlement that is named after him. His son Henry, who had moved away because of his dissatisfaction with farm life and because of an intensely antagonistic relationship with his father, has returned after his marriage. Lovise, the daughter, is in love with Olaf Nelson, the son of a poor prairie farmer. Jens Braastad used to object so strongly to this relationship that he tolerated the attempt of Jonathan Shay, a wealthy and, in Braastad's eyes, more appropriate suitor, to break Lovise's resistance with cunning as well as force. Lovise successfully defended herself, but when she learned about the extent of her father's cooperation with Shay, she left the farm.

Braastad came to realize that his family was about to break apart and changed his tyrannical ways; thus, he was able to reunite with his children—and with his wife, who had been in treatment at a mental institution. Olaf Nelson, a strong advocate of Norwegian culture, left for his first trip to the land of his ancestors. Before his departure, he and Lovise cleared up the misunderstandings that had arisen between them and made plans for a common future.

At this point, the story of *Frihetens hjem* commences. The settlement is transformed when a real estate agency sells land to new settlers. Some of them are of British stock; others, though Norwegian, have been completely assimilated into the American mainstream. These newcomers lack any appreciation for the Norwegian traditions of the township and object vehemently to the use of the Norwegian language by the original settlers. A new spirit of Americanism permeates the district. The Braastads, and in particular their new member Olaf Nelson, are staunch defenders of the old ways.

Frihetens hjem contains several parallel plot lines. It describes life in a North Dakota settlement at the time of World War I, relates the experiences of the Braastad clan, and tries to provide insights into attitudes concerning America's participation in the war. The most important topical focus of the novel, however, centers on the development of Norwegian cultural identity in the United States. Is it possible to be a good American and a good Norwegian at the same time? The contemporary political debate inspired Johnson to a comprehensive examination of this question.

Simon Johnson did not approach the issue of Norwegian-American identity from the standpoint of a disengaged observer; he was personally involved in this discussion and wanted to support cultural preservation. How did Johnson try to transmit his message? The answer can be found in the development of the novel's major characters, because the opposition of "good versus bad" coincides with the opposition of "pro-Norwegian versus anti-Norwegian." This dichotomy of pro-Norwegian role models and unattractive anti-Norwegian characters is Johnson's primary device to convince the reader.

In addition to the role played by the contrast of characters, the story line in itself reflects on the issue of Norwegian-American identity. When Olaf Nelson writes from Norway, he conveys to Lovise the peculiar emotions that permeate him when he walks upon the paths of their common forefathers or visits places where his family has dwelt and made a living. He describes the beauty of the landscape and concludes:

> I have experienced two great things in my life; one is your love, the other is my stay in Norway. And as I walk around here with the melancholy of farewell in my thoughts, there is nothing I wish more for each bright youth of Norwegian descent in America than such a love and such a journey to Norway. It cannot but increase their desire for everything that is beautiful and pure.[1]

Not everyone shares Olaf's feelings about Norway. Jerome Audobon Mostead greets Lovise in English and insists on calling her Miss Braystead, but his appearance and his arguments are described in such a laughable manner that he serves as little more than a background against which to contrast the young woman's sound answers. Lovise defends the use of Norwegian in town and church, while the novel's narrator actively supports her by praising her answers.

Back in North Dakota, Olaf asserts that the Norwegian immigrants have failed America by needlessly discarding much of their heritage instead of sharing it with their new country. Interrogated by Mostead about his reasons for visiting the little country of Norway instead of one of the larger European nations, the returned traveler explains that Norway is the land of his ancestors and of both historical and cultural significance. Olaf sees people like Mostead, who have severed all ties with the old country, as mere parrots of their new neighbors. In spite of his unpleasant experiences with the Norwegian upper class, Jens Braastad shares Olaf's reservations about people of Norwegian stock who denigrate their Norwegian heritage.

Olaf and Lovise get married and move into their new house, in which they furnish an "Olaf Nelson and Lovise Braastad room" as their personal and cultural refuge. Olaf recites Norwegian literature to his wife, for example Bjørnson's *Bergljot;* Lovise plays works by Edvard Grieg, but also the American anthem, on the piano.

The years before World War I experience a flourishing of Norwegian-American culture. The immigrants have established themselves; they have sufficient time and money to think about non-material values. Universities and high schools add Norwegian to their curricula; ethnic associations are founded. The centennial of the Norwegian constitution in 1914 marks the highlight of these activities, and Jens Braastad partakes in its celebration. His happy childhood memories outweigh the dissatisfaction he experienced in later years, and he and Lovise undertake a journey to the old country, until the outbreak of the European war necessitates their immediate return. Lovise feels pride in being a Norwegian-American, in having drawn strength from a land like Norway to use in a land like the United States.

Populism sweeps over North Dakota, and Olaf opposes the movement. Among other aspects, he dislikes the fact that the new political discussion diverts people from traditional cultural activities. Jonathan Shay draws attention to Olaf's Norwegian orientation when the Populist party leaders wonder about the latter's absence from the organization's ranks and suggests that Olaf would turn America into a Norwegian province. Olaf worries about the preservation of the immigrant heritage, because he perceives the frailty of this exposed culture. When Lovise questions the preservability of something so fragile, Olaf replies that the most precious things tend to be the most delicate ones as well.

The pressure on the various immigrant groups increases with the growing involvement of the United States in the war in Europe. Olaf compares the increasing intolerance toward ethnic minorities in the United States with the intolerance blamed on Germany. Some of his articles on this topic are printed in a brochure that wins Olaf some renown in Norwegian-American circles. He objects to the increasing demands to shed all non-English cultural and personal affinities, to the campaign against "hyphenated" Americans. Criticizing the fact that renouncing fathers, mothers, and ancestors in general is called patriotism, he fears that the intense pressure to conform will damage the spiritual life of Norwegian America.

When the United States enters the war, Henry Braastad volunteers, yet people who speak a foreign language continue to be regarded with suspicion. Arne Arneson, one of the early settlers in the area, refers to the Norwegian pioneers who died cultivating the prairies as the little army the Norwegians have already furnished in the past; they have nothing to be ashamed of for honoring their own language. Olaf is put in charge of the local war effort and visits the farms in the district. When an old Norwegian farmer addresses Olaf in his mother tongue, Chester Blowe, an American of British descent who assists in the collection of war contributions, scolds the man for being a friend of the German emperor and demands an end to the use of foreign gibberish in America. Olaf reiterates that the attempt to force the national language upon people who speak other tongues is an expression of the "German spirit" America is fighting.

Blowe and his friends Blaise Poppen and Jerome Audobon Mostead are furious because so many people speak Norwegian in the settlement; they even teach it to their children, who grow up as foreigners. Blowe suggests repatriation to Norway, whereas Poppen would prefer the use of dynamite. Mostead categorizes the failure to relinquish foreign ways as ingratitude toward the generous country that offered them refuge. The patriots decide that Olaf Nelson is a Norwegian, not an American, and resolve to teach him a lesson that demonstrates the sentiments held by true Americans. Reflecting on the support they receive from Jonathan Shay, who comes from a Norwegian family but is married to an American woman, they reach the conclusion that only regular contact with real Americans can Americanize foreigners.

Olaf learns about their designs and confronts some of the conspirators, yet at the same time, his devotion to the United States becomes stronger rather than weaker. He reasons that he is not surrounded by true Americans—an idea he shares with his opponents—and that the true American spirit dwells in other places. His negative experiences, therefore, do not diminish his praise of America's unique war effort or his dedication to writing exaltedly patriotic poems.

Lovise takes one of his poems as an occasion to give vent to her feelings. She is deeply touched by the experience of America's great power and by her brother Henry's death for this country and begins to question the feasibility of raising her children as Norwegians in the United States—considering the forces of society and the peer pressure the children would be exposed to. Olaf's counterarguments are already muted. He reiterates his deep-felt Americanism, but he demands that it ought to be possible in a free country to draw from the history and the literature of one's ethnic group.

In order to respond to the suspicions that have been cast upon his interest in Norway, Olaf invites an independent outside commission to examine his conduct and the attacks upon him. He maintains that his exploration of that country and its culture contributed to his spiritual growth, because a person's self-respect is enhanced by knowledge and acceptance of his heritage. If people cannot be honorable toward themselves, they cannot honor their country either. At the same time, Olaf explained, his exposure to Norwegian culture had deepened his interest in American culture. In case of a war between Norway and the United States, he would be faithful to his new country, although it would anguish him to fight against his own relatives.

Olaf's adversaries cannot prevail over this testimony. Chester Blowe argues that native-born Americans possess an innate feeling for what is American, something that cannot be attained by foreigners. Those who speak their own languages ought to be returned to where they came from. If the law does not allow for dealing appropriately with such persons, true Americans have traditionally put themselves above the dead letter of the law. Blowe's and Poppen's testimonies fail to impress the commissioner, and Olaf Nelson is given another opportunity to present his views on the cultural question:

> We really have to be adult enough to distinguish between the nation's life and the cultural treasures that belong to everyone. For many, this is a fairly easy affair. An Englishman who becomes an American citizen is not attacked if he feels like integrating English intellectual life into his own. Why? Because these treasures come in the language that is used by the majority here in this country—the country's official language. The same thing is the case with the Irish and the Scottish—and for the same reason. If they try to hand down the treasures they have acquired this way to their children, no one questions their national spirit for that reason. But if I employ the same self-evident right, I become an object of suspicion and hate, even though I approach my civil duties as conscientiously as my private affairs. Why this distinction? Is American law not strong enough to grant the same rights to the descendants of the Vikings as to the de-

scendants of English immigrants? If not—then the country and the people lose stature, not those who use their legal and human rights. . . .[2]

Olaf is cleared and embarks on a successful career. He defends the rights of immigrants, but time moves on. A new pastor comes to the settlement and conducts most of his business in English. The old generation, which was still born in Norway, passes away, and to their grandchildren Norwegian is a thing of the past.

Simon Johnson was no man of subtleties. His novel was meant to demonstrate to his fellow Norwegian-Americans that it was neither in their nor in America's best interest if they abandoned their heritage. The creation and development of his characters is subject to furthering this message. This results in a correlation of positive character traits and positive attitudes toward Norwegian culture and between negative character traits and negative attitudes toward Norwegian culture. Even Henry Braastad's position as the only member of the Braastad clan with weak bonds to his Norwegian ancestry is paralleled by his rather average strength of character. He is a man of good intentions who cannot overcome his weaknesses. In the political sphere, he has assimilated into the prevailing American culture without actively denouncing Norwegian traditions. The other main characters are positioned clearly on their respective sides of the fence—the good one or the bad one. As the book narrates the story of the Braastad clan, the protagonists are on the good side and assume a dominant position as far as character development and spatial allotment are concerned.

Olaf Nelson is the main protagonist in *Frihetens hjem* and represents Johnson's ideal of a Norwegian-American man. He is the son of a poor prairie farmer who did not succeed in the New World, thereby exemplifying the counterpart to Jens Braastad—not all emigrants strike it rich in America. Olaf is an avid reader and begins to surpass his peers intellectually. He falls in love with Lovise Braastad, the daughter of the wealthiest farmer in the area. She seems like an unattainable princess—not without reason, since her father nearly succeeds in driving the couple apart.

His journey to Norway is a dream come true for Olaf, who has been an ardent proponent of Norwegian culture all his life and thoroughly enjoys the opportunity to see the country personally. He travels to many places, visits relatives and family friends, and never forgets to send letters to Lovise that express his love for her and for his two homelands.

After his return, Olaf is confronted with the recent arrivals and with the new spirit they have brought to Braastad. He opposes both the Populist movement and the unfolding loyalty campaign, which stigmatizes Norwegian traditions. When Olaf is put in charge of the local war effort, he is given an opportunity to retaliate against his adversaries, but he never considers abusing his power. Instead, he relishes the temporary peace within the settlement that the war outside has brought forth and writes idyllic poems to his wife in his spare time. When he learns of incriminations against him, he requests that they be investigated by an independent commission. During this inquiry, he convincingly presents his position that one can be a good American and preserve respect for one's heritage at the same time.

Olaf is described as a knight in shining armor. He is a devoted husband who explains the world's mysteries to his attentively listening wife, a successful farmer, a connoisseur of music and literature, a man who triumphs over his enemies but always forgives them, and a man who is faithful to his ancestral heritage and still 150 percent American. He was meant to be an example to Norwegian-Americans and express the views the author wanted his audience to adopt.

Lovise Braastad is drawn as a model wife. One has to keep this in mind when judging the use of character development in Johnson's textual structure. The modern reader will find amusing aspects in Lovise's admiration for Olaf, particularly the embarrassing bluntness with which she expresses it. The author did not intend these characteristics to be humorous but regarded them as exemplary. He explained Lovise's weaker character as an expression of her femininity. Interestingly, Johnson created a more independent female character in Henry Braastad's wife Mary, who does not, however, play a role in the language debate.

Jens Braastad—the *pater familias*, the cotter turned rich farmer—undergoes the most surprising change of all the characters in the previous novel, *Fallitten paa Braastad*. In that book he starts out as the tyrannical patriarch who alienates his wife and children, but at the beginning of *Frihetens hjem*, he has become a positive figure, supporting his family and the Norwegian cause. He aids Olaf in his struggle against both forced assimilation and Populism.

Lisa Braastad lived in her strong husband's shadow for a long time. She underwent extensive treatment in a mental institution. When she finally recovers, she spends her last years quietly and peacefully on the farm. Whereas she grew up in Norway, her grandchildren are third-generation Americans, and Lovise realizes the discontinuation of traditions when she notices how her children no longer understand their grandmother's lullabies.

Arne Arneson came to America with Olaf's father. He is fond of Olaf and devoted to his Norwegian heritage. When Jonathan Shay incites the local Populists against the Braastad clan, Arneson, although a party member, visits Olaf and informs him of the rumors that are afloat. He is always levelheaded and above party lines, and the fact that he is described very favorably, in spite of his Populist views, indicates that the ethnic debate was more important to the author than the political debate.

Pastor Bry arrives in town during the war. A dignified old man, he has been working on the frontier all his life. When a newspaper publishes a letter attacking him for having studied German theology and for preaching in Norwegian, the congregation is engulfed in a dramatic dispute. Although a vast majority supports him, the pastor wants to resign because he cannot bear the thought that he could alienate people enough to break with the Church. Before he can turn in his letter of resignation, he dies at his desk.

Opposite these role models, Johnson has placed an array of negative characters who attempt to subvert the preservation of Norwegian culture in the community. Their preeminent representative is Jonathan Shay. He is the son of wealthy Norwegian-American farmers, but he and his family ascribe no value to their heritage and assimilate into Yankee culture in order to climb socially. Pursuing Lovise as a way to combine the two adjacent farms, Shay develops an insatiable thirst for revenge when she rejects him for Olaf Nelson. In order to be wed before Lovise, he hastily proposes to a young socialite, and as a Populist politician he abuses his influence to incite hostility against the Braastads among the party faithful. When Olaf writes a confidential letter to the party's headquarters, in which he explains his objections to its policies, Shay has it circulated in the settlement and manages to arouse negative feelings against his rival. In spite of his own Norwegian background, Shay has no qualms about denouncing Olaf's pride in his heritage. Yet when the commission investigating Olaf examines Shay's role, he distances himself from his fellow conspirators and denies having had any part in the plan to teach Olaf a lesson.

Jerome Audobon Mostead is one of the newcomers who intend to bring enlightenment to the settlement. He never mentions his Norwegian parents, whose name was Mostad, and agitates against the use of Norwegian in the community. In Mostead's eyes, Britain represents the origin of all liberty and the jewel among nations. His former profession as a schoolmaster is easy to discern, even though he moved west in search of an idealized rural lifestyle. Mostead expects immigrants to America to show their gratitude toward the new country by breaking from their old ways as quickly as possible.

Matias Mastlie, who calls himself Marx Glibb Masterley, has expressed his internationalism through the choice of his name. He objects to political and ethnic boundaries, calling them inventions of the capitalists and the warlords. Masterley is waiting for the world revolution or, as an alternative, for the time when he has made twenty thousand dollars and can begin a life of travel. His neglected farm will never be able to yield such a high profit, so the new political movement offers him a different route. He becomes a major agitator for the Populists, whose leaders value his oratorical skills, and gladly abandons agriculture in favor of a political career.

Blaise Poppen was brought to Braastad by the real estate agency. He is a Yankee, a veteran of the Spanish War, and a fierce opponent of everything foreign. A little man with a stiff leg as a war memento, he feels called to guard America against Norwegian influences. This attitude makes him a useful instrument in Jonathan Shay's campaign against Olaf Nelson. He contends that he will not retreat from a gibberish-preacher such as Olaf, considering that he had not retreated from the Spaniards. Easily incited to the idea of teaching Olaf a lesson, he wants him tried by the popular justice of real Americans such as himself and Chester Blowe. The latter is equally adverse to the use of foreign languages and demands that the true American spirit must prevail, a spirit to which his descent from an English grandfather in Illinois grants him a special claim. He admits to Olaf that he was planning to give him a "reminder" of the fact that they were in the United States and not in Norway, but his views about the true American spirit, real Americans, and popular justice during the investigation of Olaf Nelson's activities infuriate the judge sufficiently to contemplate legal action against him.

* * *

Frihetens hjem is a didactic novel with a ubiquitous political intent. This political intent creates artistic problems. How can the author make his message clear and convincing to a larger audience without compromising his art? Politics and art use a different form of discourse, and some of the story's formal weaknesses can be ascribed to this difference. Johnson wanted to make sure the message would emerge clearly.

Norwegian-American writers of that time tended to have experience with didactic fiction. Simon Johnson and many others had been active in the Prohibition movement, and their educational writings against "Satan Alcohol" influenced their style. An ever-present narrator—actively participating in the story and praising or criticizing the characters—is a comparatively heavy-handed device and constituted a fairly outdated narrative technique, even at that time.

The clear-cut separation between good and evil, which portrays likable characters as holding the correct political views and their adversaries as both politically and personally flawed, represents a further aspect of the novel's didacticism. While artistically dissatisfying, the political impact on the average reader may have been enhanced by it; moral relativism can confuse people.

Sometimes the spirit of the time can become tiresome. The moral supremacy expressed toward the war enemy, Germany, combined with a somewhat simplistic view of international politics might seem a little naive now; yet, it contributes to the work's historical authenticity. The views expressed were those held at that time, and the novel involuntarily preserves them. The immigrant writer, faced with accusations of foreign allegiances by a nativist popular mood, feels compelled to outdo his accusers. The deep impact of the antiforeign campaign of these years becomes obvious in the passionate claims of patriotism that permeate the works of immigrant writers.

As a consequence of this lack of detachment, the contemporary relevance of the novel changes. Its artistic quality suffers, but its value as a document increases. Perhaps it was only appropriate for a writer like Simon Johnson to achieve a place in cultural history less as an author of great literary works than as a chronicler of his time.

4
Hans Rønnevik's Answer to the Loyalism Campaign

Hans Rønnevik was born in the southwestern Norwegian coastal town of Haugesund in 1887. Following his emigration to America in 1905, he initially worked on a farm in Minnesota. He attended Augsburg Seminary in Minneapolis in 1907–1908 and taught at a Norwegian parochial school in South Dakota. After homesteading in Montana, he married the Norwegian-American Nillie Tysver in 1914 and found a lasting home in Carlisle, Minnesota.

Rønnevik remained a farmer by profession and published only one novel, *100 procent* (100 Percent). For this book, which appeared in 1926, he shared the literature prize of The Norwegian Society of America with Thor Helgeson in the following year. He contributed to various Norwegian publications in the United States and in Norway—among them *Ved Lampelys, Nordisk Tidende,* and *Haugesund Dagblad*—and continued to write literary works, although he could not find a publisher for them. An unpublished novel called *Per og meg* (Per and I) revolves around two old men reminiscing about their lives. Another, *Paradis* (Paradise), describes a Norwegian settlement in Southern Minnesota.[1] Rønnevik visited Norway several times during his life, which lasted well beyond World War II. He died in Carlisle in 1962.

100 procent takes place in a Minnesota town during the First World War. The protagonist is a young Norwegian-American who changes his name from Louis Olson to his grandfather's Lars Holte. He lives on the family's farm, but when his widowed father marries the housekeeper, life becomes so unbearable for Lars that he moves to town to seek his fortune.

The outbreak of the war in Europe produces strong tensions in the area because the native-born population views itself as an outpost of true Americanism in an environment of disloyal foreigners. Furthermore, these old-stock Americans are the leaders of the Republican Party, which has come under attack from the emerging protest movement of the Nonpartisan League (NPL). In their eyes, their various opponents form a single group that engages in multiple un-American activities: opposition to America's entry into the war—in their mind "Kaiserism"; and agricultural protest—in their words "socialism."

Lars likes some of the Populist ideas but regards the NPL as too radical and too ruthless in its methods. Even though he is critical of the German government, he opposes the propagandistic efforts by which the Allies and their supporters attempt to incite the American population against Germany and the Germans. These viewpoints suffice to make him a target when America moves toward war and the regional political leadership openly resorts to coercive measures against the NPL and other opposition.

* * *

When Louis Olson changes his name, he reverses the step taken by his father, who did not want to bear an outmoded, foreign name. Andrew Olson, a conservative Republican opposed to anything that appears radical, disapproves of his son's decision, whereas Lars does not perceive his action as offensive to anyone. He does not view it as directed against the United States; indeed, he feels that the dignity of his ancestral name represents a superior kind of Americanism. This is important to him, because he regards the United States as the greatest country in the world. His brief attendance at a Norwegian-language college has increased his awareness of being a *Norwegian* American, without decreasing his American patriotism.

The reaction to Lars's newly expressed ethnic awareness is mixed. Many people are surprised at the puzzling step taken by this hitherto exemplary young man. His generational peers, more pragmatically, fail to see its point. Lars, according to them, will be changed to Louis in American mouths anyway. There are those who congratulate Lars, such as the widow Guri Brenden. Although she too is convinced of America's unique qualities, her five sons all bear Norwegian names in honor of their heritage. The former seminarian Thormod Kvinnesdal feels less need to be thankful to America, because the fact that the Norwegians settled and developed this part of the country should, in his opinion, have earned *them* gratitude. Thormod wants Norwegian culture and language to occupy the most honored place in this new "Normandy." At sixty years of age, he shows no signs of giving up his struggle for a Norwegian America in spite of the disappointments it entails. Finally, Lars finds approval with Olaus Nilsen, whose role as a political outsider has earned him the name "the Democrat," and who is held in low regard by the townspeople.

Whereas Lars does not place much value in praise from Olaus Nilsen, he is all the more interested in the views of Inga Vang, Nilsen's niece, who has recently arrived from Norway. When they become acquainted, Lars shares the motivation behind his name change with her and explains that it by no means expressed a desire to be more Norwegian than American. Lars also erects a tall flagpole, the only private one in the area, which arouses the suspicion not only of the neighbors but also of his own father. When he hoists a large American banner on the fourth of July, however, the official speaker lauds the patriotism expressed by the impressive flag in front of the hillside farmhouse. The very same night, the flagpole is cut down by his father's housekeeper and future wife, Annie, who is upset by Lars and his outlandish ideas. Lars leaves the farm and moves to town, where he marries Inga and soon owns the lumber store in which he first found work.

The town is inhabited by people of many backgrounds. In addition to the dominant Norwegian element, there are Germans and Swedes, a group of blacks who had been recruited by the banker Edward Stone and whose economic dependency on him makes them his most reliable supporters, and last but by no means least, a small number of old-stock Americans. They see themselves as the only true Americans, destined to be in charge of the settlement. Besides Edward Stone, George Smith, landowner and mayor, is the most prominent member of the Yankee establishment. Although he is of Norwegian descent and employs his background when it benefits his business interests, Pete Harmsen, owner of the town's other bank, strives to become part of this elite circle. Because he attempts to be everything to everybody, as long as his business stands to profit from it, people have started to refer to him as "Pete Harmsen, at your service."

Another notable citizen is Pastor Johnson, who is determined to Anglicize his church as rapidly as possible in spite of his Norwegian roots. His difficulties with Norwegian as a newly arrived seminarian had contributed to his orientation toward English, and the meager livelihood he earned as the pastor of a Norwegian Free Church in North Dakota only intensified his desire for a comfortable, respected, American position. To his dismay, the economically important older generation in his new congregation still insists on the frequent use of its mother tongue, but Pastor Johnson steadfastly works to achieve

Hans Rønnevik.
Courtesy family Hans A. Rønnevik, Carlisle, Minnesota.

his goal. He gradually increases the percentage of English used in his church and waits for an opportunity to discontinue Norwegian services.

Pastor Johnson's attitude toward the presence of the Norwegian language in the Lutheran Church is shared by many pastors, particularly the younger ones. At first, most of the immigrant churches and schools used Norwegian, but the old leaders increasingly have been replaced by people who do not share their ideals. Third-generation Norwegian-Americans grow up knowing little about the land of their ancestors or even about their own families. Only from such Norwegian-born pioneers as Thormod Kvinnesdal can Lars and Inga learn about the settlement's development and about the history of the Norwegian people in both the new country and the old.

When the First World War breaks out in Europe, its repercussions are felt even in this remote American prairie town where people follow the exciting events in the newspapers and openly discuss the distant developments. Increasingly, however, biased press reports undermine the democratic openness of the war debates, as supporters of American military intervention attempt to incense the public with questionable accounts of alleged German atrocities. Lars, who looks at the events in Europe with complete impartiality, becomes dismayed at the rapidly intensifying propaganda efforts against the German people both in Europe and in America. When Midwestern senators such as La Follette of Wisconsin and Gronna of North Dakota manage to delay America's entry into the war through a filibuster, emotions flare on both sides. In spite of the activities of Edward Stone and his followers, most of the people assembled to wait for the outcome of the senate debate—among them many Germans from the farming areas surrounding the town—welcome the news of La Follette's temporary success. Pastor Johnson becomes so enraged that he knocks down Thormod Kvinnesdal with his gold-trimmed cane, and only Lars's intervention saves him from the outraged crowd.

The resistance of a few senators produces only a short reprieve. America's declaration of war gives momentum and increased official support to the patriotic hard-liners, who have long been dismayed by the lack of enthusiasm for the war displayed by the area's population. Without daring to resist, many immigrants resent the war propaganda and the increasing pressure to conform; yet others, among them Guri Brenden's youngest son, Sverre, enthusiastically respond to the country's appeal to their patriotism and enlist.

The patriotic fervor claims its first victims. Pete Harmsen changes

4: HANS RØNNEVIK'S ANSWER TO THE LOYALISM CAMPAIGN

the name of his bank from "Scandinavian American State Bank" to "Midland American Bank." Having selected the original name for business purposes, he no longer regards it an asset. The banker receives many compliments for this action, but he loses the accounts of Lars and other prominent customers, who are indignant about Harmsen's contention that there is no longer room for foreign names in America. Whereas the Scandinavians, whose homelands are not even at war with the United States, slip away with this minor insult, the Germans have to pay a heavier price. Under the leadership of Edward Stone, a patriotic mob changes the name of "Bismarck Avenue" to "Washington Avenue," in the process throwing an effigy of the late German chancellor into the river. An old German woman who frantically protests their action barely escapes the same fate.

Not only the war but also the appearance of the Nonpartisan League creates tensions during these years. This prairie protest movement wins the elections in North Dakota and spreads rapidly into Minnesota. Suspicious of the trusts and financial institutions that control the welfare of the farmers, the party looks critically at the interventionist drive that seems to find its strongest backers in the same circles. Many German and Scandinavian farmers support the movement, which severely threatens the regional political and economic establishment. The latter, therefore, uses the patriotically charged mood of the country to brand the NPL as disloyal and consisting of socialists and "Kaiserists." Nevertheless, many local people join the new party. Among them is Thormod Kvinnesdal, who also tries to recruit Lars. Although he agrees with some of the Populist ideas and with the NPL's opposition to certain aspects of wartime patriotism, Lars does not share his friend's enthusiasm for the party and alludes to the demagoguery to which it, too, has been resorting.

Guri Brenden convinces Lars to start a Norwegian youth club. When all the invited young people congregate at Guri's place, Lars describes the purpose of their gathering: they need to preserve the great heritage of their ancestors, and it will be to America's advantage if they succeed. The participants respond enthusiastically, and the new club begins its activities, which consist of lectures, literature readings, and debates, always followed by a cozy social hour. Retired Pastor Bakke becomes a regular guest at the meetings. He had acceded to the prevalent view that Norwegian traditions were doomed and could not be saved, but his experiences with these young people demonstrate to him that he was mistaken. Pastor Johnson disapproves of his predecessor's participation in this nonreligious and, moreover, "foreign" organization, but Bakke defends the club and retorts by suggesting that the expansion of Norwegian activities might actually lead to an increase in church attendance.

Johnson decides that drastic action is called for and instigates a mob attack on youth club members returning from a picnic. The atmosphere in the country has become so hostile toward everything regarded as foreign that the club has kept a low profile—to no avail. An incensed crowd awaits the young Norwegian-Americans with buckets of yellow paint, but a tempestuous storm defeats their plans, and they end up with more paint on themselves than on their intended targets.

In his church, the pastor works toward removing all remnants of the Norwegian language. He organizes a festive meeting for the district's young people, which is to be the first of its kind that is held exclusively in English. Toward the end of the event he introduces a resolution to be presented to the synod, in which he demands the omission of the word Norwegian from its official name. When his attempts to inveigle the gathering into supporting his resolution are thwarted by Lars, Pastor Johnson concludes that the latter is the driving force behind the disloyal activities in the area.

War requires money, and the government asks the people for war loans, but there is nothing voluntary about these contributions. Loan drive committees estimate the amount expected from each individual. People have little choice but to fulfill their quota, even if they must borrow the money required. Lars, who serves on such a committee, rejects Pete Harmsen's method of demanding money and insists on politely requesting contributions; the banker notes this as an expression of lukewarm support for the war. When Lars is confronted with Harmsen's accounts of heinous German atrocities and discovers that these rumors are based on misrepresentations spread by a traveling propaganda speaker, he finally explodes and bitterly assails the misguided form of patriotism that expresses itself in the name of 100 percent Americanism.

The immigrants are regarded with suspicion, yet they are good enough to serve in the military. All of Guri Brenden's sons are drafted, and even Lars's new employee Erik Lønning, who has not yet acquired American citizenship, is called to arms. The common people fulfill their duty, whereas some of the influential patriots seem to find a way around the hardships of wartime life. Lars is torn because he resents the propaganda and the attacks on everything foreign but deeply desires to support the country he holds in such high esteem. When

4: HANS RØNNEVIK'S ANSWER TO THE LOYALISM CAMPAIGN 63

President Wilson publishes his Fourteen Points to end the war, Lars backs the president's proposals and even considers volunteering for military service.

One event changes his plans—and his life—forever. Pastor Johnson and Pete Harmsen feel called to salvage the reputation of the Upper Midwest, which has supplied the leading figures of the antiwar movement, by enticing a mob to hang North Dakota Senator Gronna in effigy. Lars is appalled when late one night he encounters a large crowd assembled under a giant gallows. A speaker accuses the many immigrants in the area of sympathizing with the enemy and pronounces the death sentence for one of them, the "traitor" Senator Gronna. When they try to hang the senator's effigy, Lars rushes toward the gallows, cuts through the rope, and disappears. The next morning he is arrested.

In the trial against Lars, his enemies list his transgressions. Not only has he changed his name, but he also prefers the Norwegian language to English and has founded a youth club that celebrates foreign ideals. He has opposed Pastor Johnson's attempts to Americanize his church, and his purported membership in the new party further confirms his disloyalty. The testimony of his friends counts little against these accusations by the town's leading personalities, and Lars is sentenced to ninety days in prison.

While Lars serves his jail term, the loyalist campaign of intimidation, directed mainly against the Nonpartisan League, continues to unfold. One of the League's speakers is tarred and feathered, the editor of their newly founded paper is severely beaten, and their printing press is destroyed. Thormod Kvinnesdal reports these events to Lars when, at last, he is allowed to see him in prison. Andrew Olson visits his son as well and apologizes for the wrongs he has committed against him. Lars forgives him, but he shows little concern for the future of the family farm. His thoughts have already moved on.

The war finally ends. Guri Brenden has lost all her sons except Sverre, who returns broken in body and spirit. He and Erik Lønning have learned to hate the war and everything connected with it. Wilson's Fourteen Points remain theory, ignored by the triumphant Allies in Europe. The wartime commotion in the settlement continues even beyond the armistice and only gradually dies down. Lars Holte, however, no longer cares. He has given up on America, on the country that he loved so dearly and by which he feels so bitterly betrayed. His wife, Inga, is overjoyed when he announces his intention to move to Norway with her and their son and to settle on her family's farm.

They sail to Norway, gazing back at the country they leave behind while they stand on deck with Guri and Sverre Brenden and Erik Lønning, who are all bound for the same destination.

* * *

There is general agreement that World War I represented a severe challenge to the future of Norwegian America, and several novels portray its impact on this community. Nowhere is the war so central to the understanding of the atmosphere of the time as in Hans Rønnevik's book, however. The short period from 1912 to 1919 sees the cataclysmic events of the war debate and of the political upheaval caused by the agrarian protest movement. Even though both of these developments were of universal significance and represented national issues beyond the scope of Norwegian America, they soon became interconnected with each other and with the ethnic question. The excesses of contemporary American nationalism, marked by a deep fear of immigrant disloyalty, clarified the Anglo-American expectation of complete immigrant assimilation. At the same time, the strong representation of Scandinavians and Germans in the agrarian protest movement—based originally on the sheer demographic fact that the majority of the Upper Midwestern farm population descended from these peoples—was intensified by the political attacks directed at both farmers and immigrants. The German element, originally less inclined to support radical protest to the same extent as did many Scandinavians, increasingly regarded the Populists as the sole voice against harassment from the Anglo-American majority. The Nonpartisan League tried to avoid being equated with noninterventionism and neutralism, but the sentiments of many of its supporters and, even more so, the skillful attempts of the economic establishment to redirect the political debate from economic to loyalty issues contributed to the blurring of distinctions.

100 procent explores the different strategies employed by a number of Norwegian-Americans in this situation. Pete Harmsen, who stressed his ethnic background when it seemed lucrative, drops the last vestiges of Norwegian ethnicity and actively supports the loyalists. He is joined by Pastor Johnson, who is indignant at his congregation's resistance to total assimilation and uses the wartime atmosphere to achieve his linguistic goals. On the other end of the spectrum, Thormod Kvinnesdal consistently opposes established viewpoints both in cultural and in economic questions. He argues that the Norwegians have earned the right to their own culture by cultivating the prairie and that they need not sacrifice their identity to express their gratitude to America. Kvinnesdal combines this cultural preservationism with wholehearted activism on the side of the NPL and with opposition to the war.

Rønnevik elucidates the role of outright coercion in the assimilation process. While the American political elites generally relied on the influence of time and social environment to accomplish the Anglicization of the newcomers and treated immigrant cultures with benevolent neglect, they did not refrain from more violent means in times of perceived crisis. Of special interest is the role of native American authority figures in this process. In prairie settlements, these interspersed Yankees long maintained social power beyond their numerical strength. In the midst of increasing numbers of immigrants, they grew into a role of both missionaries and viceroys of American society, who defended their lifestyle and their economic position at the same time. In their struggle, they were aided by assimilated immigrants, who felt the need to underscore their commitment to Americanism. The latter were embarrassed by the more foreign elements within their ethnic groups, who perpetuated the negative stereotypes about those groups in American society at large. Not only did assimilated immigrants shed their own foreign ways, but they also propagated the participation of their ancestral community in this process. This was necessary because even acculturated immigrants could not easily escape being identified with the group from which they had sprung.

Wartime patriots opposed "hyphenated" Americans and demanded "100 percent Americanism." Whereas the American political leadership had been content with political loyalty up to that point and had largely tolerated cultural and linguistic diversity, the atmosphere of World War I equated the use of languages other than English with continued allegiance to the countries in which these languages had their origin. The recurring descriptions of the stigmatization of foreign language use and of the psychological impact of the loyalism campaign on the immigrants reassert the importance that World War I had for the rapidity of the decline in Norwegian language retention. The counterarguments that point to the underlying weaknesses present in the immigrant community, and to the fact that only part of the language switch actually took place during the time of the most intensive pressure, cannot diminish the significance of the psychological damage wreaked within the immigrant community. The accusations of disloyalty and the painful social repercussions that resulted from the use of foreign languages during the antiforeign campaign induced many immigrants to reevaluate the relative advantages of the languages at their disposal and burdened the difficult position of non-English languages with additional, political considerations.

Many native-born Americans denounced the immigrants' adherence to their native culture as ungrateful, since the United States had granted them freedom from the oppression in the old country. This argument touches on an important aspect of the American public self-image, namely, the deeply held belief that immigrants flock to the United States because of the political freedom and the superior political system the country supplies. While such considerations were important to ethnic and religious minorities, they were less central to other groups. Most immigrants came for economic reasons, and seldom was this fact more pronounced than in the Northern European colonization of the Great Plains. The westward expansion of the United States offered opportunities to the land-hungry European peasant population that were unheard of in Europe. Even the best political system in the Old World could not have created conditions competitive with the enormous amounts of virtually free farm land offered in the American West. The land and the resources made available by the conquest of a continent represented America's foremost attraction. "The Norwegians came for land, not for riches," is Rønnevik's assured contribution to this discussion.

In *100 procent,* the political and economic establishment is confronted with ethno-cultural and political opposition. These two circles of resistance overlap to a certain extent, and they definitely overlap in the eyes of their opponents. In principle, however, they represent two distinct causes. Two of the leading Norwegian cultural pluralists, Lars Holte and Guri Brenden, harbor negative feelings toward the Nonpartisan League, which in turn tries to keep its political agenda separate from such potentially divisive issues as ethnicity and Americanism. Yet Thormod Kvinnesdal and numerous other northern European prairie farmers combine ethnic pride with political activism on the side of the NPL. As a consequence, the NPL shields ethnic activists from the most severe implications of the loyalty drive, as is demonstrated by the comparative lack of harassment directed at immigrants in NPL-ruled North Dakota.

The Church, on the other hand, fails to support the ethnic identity of its members. The contrast between the retired pastor, who sides with the preservationists, and his successor, who ranks prominently among the radical loyalists, indicates the significance of individual choice for the formulation of Church policy in those years. Pastor

Johnson made his decision in favor of assimilation early in life, and his emotional response to the wartime atmosphere corresponds to that of the native-born Americans. He uses the patriotic mood of the country to implement linguistic changes in his congregation. The pastor had been working toward the elimination of Norwegian for a long time, but only the threat of otherwise being labeled disloyal to America has finally convinced his congregation to go along with him.

Since the Church supports the American institutions in their drive to assimilate the Norwegians, the private youth club organized by Lars Holte and Guri Brenden remains as the sole defender of Norwegian cultural traditions. It provides an opportunity for the American-born younger generation to practice the Norwegian they have learned at home in a reinforcing environment and exposes young people to the history and culture of Norway.

That Rønnevik never became a well-known author might be partially contributed to his shakiness with regard to correct Norwegian. His language shows noticeable English influences, which express themselves not so much in loan-words but in idiomatic and grammatical mistakes.[2] These minor flaws would undoubtedly have been corrected if Rønnevik had not had to publish the novel by himself.

Rønnevik surpasses other Norwegian-American writers in his ability to see beyond his own group. Few scenes in the book are as touching as the descriptions of the desperation experienced by German-American farmers who have been exemplary citizens all their lives and suddenly become the targets of officially condoned rowdyism. These German immigrants, who have made the sacrifice to support the war against their country of origin, are nevertheless assailed for clinging to their customs and their language. They cannot openly express their resentment to the treatment they receive, but they gratefully support Lars Holte's business when he is imprisoned for his opposition to the loyalism campaign. When Rønnevik describes the frightened old farmers who dare not stay away from a war rally and the haggardly old woman who risks her life protesting the desecration of Bismarck's memory, he reaches his personal narrative peak. In general, Rønnevik becomes most powerful when he assails the patriotic excesses of the era. His antiwar sentiment is deeply personal: he strongly disapproves of the inflammatory rhetoric that paved the way toward America's entry into the war. *100 procent* preserves aspects of American history that clash with popular images of general freedom and tolerance.

The intensity of Rønnevik's reaction against the political climate of the war years demands a conclusion that is unusual among his fellow writers. The author allows his protagonist to turn from idealistic American patriotism to complete disillusionment. Lars Holte returns to the land of his ancestors in spite of his American birth, accompanied not only by his Norwegian-born wife but also by Guri Brenden, her son Sverre, and Erik Lønning. Sverre and Erik have been thoroughly transformed by the horrors of the battlefield, and they hold America responsible for their suffering. This remigration rarely occurs in Norwegian-American literature, even though the migration data reveal that many Norwegians actually did return to their homeland.

While Rønnevik's protagonist leaves America, the author's feelings toward the country remain ambiguous. When a cyclone destroys much of the town at the end of the novel, its inhabitants are praised for their unique sense of cooperation and mutual assistance. Rønnevik does not hold the common people of prairie America responsible for the injustices committed by the political and cultural leadership.

100 procent presents the one solution available for the defenders of Norwegian identity that has passed the test of time. Most of the descendants of the Norwegian-speaking Americans at the turn of the century have become mainstream Americans with only an emotional affinity to Norway. Attempts made to preserve a larger part of their heritage had little success. In the long run, only the return to Norway enabled Norwegian-Americans to fully remain a part of their ancestral community.

5
Wheat and Potatoes—Ethnic and Religious Differences in O. E. Rølvaag's Immigrant Trilogy

OLE EDVART RØLVAAG WAS BORN ON THE NORTHERN NORWEGIAN island of Dønna in 1876. His father was a fisherman, and the rigid societal structures of the time made it very difficult to rise above the social rank of one's family. Many Norwegians tried to escape these limitations by emigrating to America; among them was Ole Edvart, who embarked on the voyage across the Atlantic in 1896. An uncle in South Dakota loaned him the money, and this prairie state became Rølvaag's first American domicile. Initially, he worked on farms to pay off his debt, but as early as 1898 he enrolled at Augustana Academy in Canton, South Dakota. At this school and thereafter at St. Olaf College in Minnesota, both founded by Norwegian Lutherans, he developed a deep interest in a topic that would occupy him throughout his life: the fate of the Norwegian immigrants in the United States. Both as a writer and in his primary profession as a college professor, he stood in the center of the historical developments of this immigrant group. After graduating from St. Olaf and completing a year of graduate studies at the University of Oslo, he began his academic career at his American alma mater and married Jennie Berdahl, the daughter of Norwegian farmers in South Dakota. The fisherman's son had done well in the new country.

Rølvaag had always had a passion for literature. He started his first novel, *Nils og Astri* (Nils and Astri), while he was still in school, and even though he could not find a publisher for this early literary attempt, he persisted in a writing career that would eventually make him the most famous Norwegian-American author. A large part of both his fictional and his nonfictional writings examines the experiences of the Norwegian immigrant population in the United States.

Rølvaag's lifespan covered the culmination and the subsequent decline of Norwegian emigration and Norwegian-American cultural life. Around 1900, there were still aftershocks of the massive emigration in the 1880s, but by 1920 new emigration had been curtailed. The number of Norwegian-born people began to decline.

Norwegian cultural life in America blossomed during the first decades of the twentieth century, when the settlers had become established enough to spend time and money on cultural activities. The suppression of foreign languages during and after World War I, however, dealt a massive blow to many expressions of a separate Norwegian-American culture. When Rølvaag wrote his masterpiece *Giants in the Earth* and the two subsequent novels of the trilogy, whose English titles are *Peder Victorious* and *Their Fathers' God*, Norwegian life in America was on the decline.[1] Rølvaag recognized this development, and he tried to stem the tide through his fiction as he had as a college professor and as cofounder of the Norwegian-American Historical Association.

Only the last two novels of Rølvaag's immigrant trilogy will be analyzed in depth, because they represent the author's foremost literary contribution to the cultural debate raging in the Norwegian-American community. Rølvaag's cultural philosophy is more visible there than in any other of his novels.

During his last years, Rølvaag had become a famous writer with prospects of the Nobel Prize for Literature, and his son Karl was to become Governor of Minnesota. The author suffered from illness most of his life and died in Northfield at the age of fifty-five.

* * *

Giants in the Earth was originally published in Norwegian as two volumes: *I de dage* (1924, In Those Days) and *Riket grundlægges* (1925, The Founding of the Kingdom). The novel narrates the story of Per Hansa, who subsequently assumes the surname Holm. With his wife Beret and his children, he leaves the Helgeland coast in northern Norway to find a better life in the New World. The long journey ultimately takes them to the South Dakota prairie, where he breaks new land. The newcomers build sod huts, and a settlement, populated by Norwegians and Irishmen, comes into being.

Per Hansa is fascinated by the opportunities the new country has to offer. He tills his own land, a dream unattainable in Norway, and finds his life's meaning in cultivating the soil with all his energy. Severe hardships issue from harsh winters and from blizzards that

Ole Edvart Rølvaag.
Courtesy Norwegian-American Historical Association.

endanger people and livestock. Long spells of drought and massive locust swarms destroy much of the harvest, yet adversities can neither undermine Per's confidence nor impede his economic success.

Beret, on the other hand, struggles with problems her husband would never understand. Deeply embedded in religious and cultural traditions, she only abandons family and country out of love for Per Hansa. She fears the endless, treeless plain on which they have settled. What kind of place is this to live, where people dwell in sod huts, and where there are neither schools nor churches? Beret cannot cope with all the changes and disasters, and she undergoes a severe psychological crisis. Only when a newly arrived pastor becomes her counsel and she gives birth to her first American-born child, who receives the optimistic name Peder Seier (Peter Victory), does her soul find rest again.

This regained sanity is accompanied by an intense religiosity, which eventually destroys Per Hansa's life. He will have to pay the price for tearing Beret out of her familiar environment and transplanting her to this strange land, causing the mental difficulties that lead to her spiritual fanaticism. In her religious fervor, she sends Per Hansa out in a blizzard to fetch a pastor for his dying friend and neighbor Hans Olsa. *Giants in the Earth* ends with Per being found dead when the snow melts in the spring—still facing westwards in death as the eternal pioneer.

With Per Hansa dead, Beret has to assume responsibility for the farm. At the onset of *Peder Seier* (translated into English as *Peder Victorious*), the new generation has reached adolescence. Even the youngest, Peder, is in his teens and attends the American school, where Irish and Norwegian children mix. Miss Clarabelle Mahon, the teacher, is absorbed by a calling to make good Americans out of these wretched immigrant children. Her life's mission is to teach them the pure English language and thoroughly acquaint them with the glory of American history; she is appalled by the fact that the American-born children of Norwegian immigrants speak English with an accent. When she meets Beret, she advises her to discontinue the use of Norwegian in her home so that Peder's English will no longer be influenced by a foreign language, but Beret considers it more important that the boy can communicate with his mother. The pervasive Anglo-American influence in Peder's school induces Beret to transfer him to a school with a predominantly Norwegian student body on the other side of the river.

The Norwegians distinguish themselves not only from official

America, but also from the Irish Catholics with whom they share the settlement. Peder does not attribute much importance to the difference in religion and origin between the two ethnic groups and befriends Charley Doheny, the son of an Irish farmer and politician. Beret, who disapproves of the close association between Peder and the Irish, allegorically asserts that wheat and potatoes should not be kept in the same bin. By transferring her son to a different school, she hopes to increase his exposure to Norwegian influences, but the new school also requires its students to speak only English, both while they are studying and while they are playing. In Peder, whose mother knows little English and who uses Norwegian at home, this admonition creates a feeling of shame.

School proves to be the most powerful tool of assimilation. Peder knew hardly any English when he started there, but before long he begins to use this language even at home. Beret tries to counter this development by getting him involved in reading Norwegian books, but Peder is not very receptive to her suggestions. Norwegian gradually turns into a language used only for communication with Beret, whereas everything else in Peder's life is dominated by English. In particular, he is exposed to the world of the Irish. When he visits the Doheny home for the first time, he encounters a cozy mess in their living quarters; nevertheless, he rejects Beret's assertions about the distinctions between people of different descent and religion. The Irish are equally aware of their distinction from the Norwegians, however, and Peder can only stand quietly by when Doheny's friends criticize the Norwegians for keeping to themselves too much and insisting on using a language no one understands.

When Beret realizes that her children are irresistibly drawn toward American culture and are on their way toward shedding their traditions, she considers returning to Norway. She wonders if the cultural loss outweighs the benefits of their material progress, but her friend Sørine convinces her that the children would be as foreign in Norway as they themselves had been when they arrived in America. Although Beret never seriously attempts to return to Norway, her remigration phantasies betray her frustration with the cultural development in the new country.

Traditionally, the Lutheran Church formed the backbone of Norwegian ethnicity in America. Over time, the situation began to change, since new pastors no longer wanted to tie the fate of the Church to the questionable future of Norwegian cultural identity. Pastor Gabrielsen shares these notions. When he finds out that the Holm family does not possess an English Bible, he presents one to Peder. He nourishes hopes that Peder will become a pastor himself, and as such he will be called to preach the Lord's word in English. Gabrielsen predicts that the Norwegian language will be dead on the prairies in twenty years and begins to hold Bible instruction for the children in English, much to the dismay of some older members of the congregation.

When Pastor Gabrielsen preaches in English at a prayer meeting, Beret expresses her dissatisfaction. She is already indignant about the fact that Gabrielsen has given Peder the English Bible, thus condoning and furthering his assimilation process, and angrily informs the pastor that she regards it a sin to abandon one's mother tongue. Gabrielsen, always jovial, considers it a natural development for the Norwegians to exchange their ancestral tongue for the dominant language of their new country. He views attempts to prevent this process as futile and foresees no future for Norwegian in America.

Beret wonders about the pastor's predictions. Was Norwegian really going to disappear from the prairies in a few decades?

> Would it really go with them the way the pastor predicted? Could Norwegian hearts beat according to such a different sound? Would this not be death?—No, she could not understand a thing any more.—How could a sparrow adopt the song of the meadow lark and still remain a sparrow, and the cow forget that she was a cow and begin to grunt? The horses walked alongside the cows in the pasture, they were few compared with the others, but the horses did not start bellowing because of that.[2]

Pastor Gabrielsen, for his part, is dissatisfied with the development the Lutheran Church has undergone in the new country. In his eyes, the split between the young English speakers and the older Norwegian members of the congregations could have been avoided if the immigrants had founded English churches to begin with, which would also have led to a more substantial growth of the congregations.

In spite of their differences, the minister retains a high opinion of Beret Holm because he recognizes her deeply religious nature and her keen mind. He envisions Peder, who appears interested in studying theology, as his successor, but despite the pastor's pressure, Peder ultimately rejects this career path. Gabrielsen and his daughter Else, who kept Peder enthralled for awhile, disappear from his life. He wants to assume responsibility for the farm, and at his side will stand Susie, the sister of his friend Charley Doheny.

Beret's worst fears have come true—her favorite son takes a wife who is neither Norwegian nor Lutheran. Remembering how she had ignored her parents' objections by going to North America with Per Hansa, she does not fight Peder's wishes. The Irish have become part of her and her son's lives. A Catholic priest, Father Nolan, performs the wedding, and the young bride moves to the Holm farm.

Peder believes in the new America, which is going to make *e pluribus unum,* but the ethno-religious dimension cannot be ignored. The marriage becomes the talk of the town. Store Hans (Big John), Peder's brother, annoyed by constant remarks about Peder's exogamy, avoids his brother's company, and Irishmen who recognize Peder in a bar start to gossip about his marriage. Even more important are the first disagreements about religious questions between the spouses, which arise from Susie's bad conscience about her recent aloofness from the Catholic Church. For a long time, she has not visited her childhood priest, Father Williams. Peder becomes easily irritated by her anguish and displays signs of disdain for Catholic rituals. Peder has, moreover, had a confrontation with Williams over the hiring of a rainmaker, who was supposed to save the county from a devastating drought. Peder strictly opposed this sort of witchcraft and was infuriated by the priest's endorsement of the rainmaker. After Susie gives birth to a son, Williams visits her. They share a lengthy and intimate relationship, and he feels responsible for her spiritual welfare. Peder displays a long dormant hostility toward the priest, which flares up when the latter expects Peder to ensure that his wife will fulfill her religious duties. It is difficult enough for Peder to tolerate his wife's convictions, and he refuses to influence her one way or another.

In reality, he cannot even keep this neutral stance, because the spouses' religious traditions are too disparate. When Susie disapproves of laymen reading the Bible, Peder accuses the Catholic clergy of intentionally keeping the faithful uninformed in order to retain more power over them. Susie, on the other hand, blames individual reading and interpreting of the scriptures for the constant arguments and schisms within the Protestant denominations. They exchange harsh words about each other's beliefs without finding a common denominator. Peder returns to reading the Bible, and Susie goes to sleep with a rosary in her hands.

Religion is not the only factor undermining the young marriage. When Michael Doheny, Susie's father, lies sick at home, Susie moves to his farm to nurse him. Peder takes her there and is appalled by the disorder and filth. Susie is offended when he starts washing the dishes, because she has had to endure comments about the uncleanliness of the Irish before and perceives Peder's help as a silent accusation. They part irritated with one another and without deciding how long Peder will have to live without his wife and son.

Michael Doheny's condition necessitates his temporary move to town, where he stays with Father Williams; his daughter and grandson accompany him. In the atmosphere of the parsonage, Susie decides to have the child baptized without informing Peder. This issue had remained unresolved before—or so it seemed. Neither parent wanted the child to be baptized in the other faith, but unbeknownst to both of them, Beret had her friend Sørine perform a layman's baptism on her grandson. Thus, Peder Immanuel was received by the Lutheran Church. Susie knows nothing about this, so Father Williams administers the Catholic baptism on Padriac St. Olaf. Pete has two names and has been incorporated into two denominations—a visual expression of the widening rift between the spouses.

Susie goes through many difficult situations. At her father's house the jokes are on the Norwegians with their strange religion, their excessive cleanliness, and most of all, their incapability of speaking a human language—in other words, English. Michael Doheny blames his suffering on her marriage, and Father Williams reprimands her for having married outside the One True Church, thus creating dangers for the spiritual well-being of herself and her son. She does not dare to inform Peder about his son's secret baptism. She wants to see her husband, but she also feels obligated to her father. Besides, she dreads the thought of returning to the Holm farm, where she spends most of the time alone with Beret, whose determined Norwegianness and Lutheranism make any understanding impossible. Peder is gone most of the time, and even when he is at home, he converses with his mother in a language Susie cannot understand. She would like her husband to move to the Doheny farm, where they could live together with her father, away from the constricting Norwegian atmosphere at the Holm farm, but Peder rejects this idea completely.

When his wife returns to him at last, Peder has to accept some changes, since Susie insists on going to Mass more often and decorates the house with a crucifix, a holy water font, and a book about the life of the saints. Peder is taken aback, and although he initially avoids a confrontation, his recurrent deriding of Catholic beliefs causes new arguments. During her second pregnancy, Susie tells her husband about her prayers for a girl, but Peder ridicules her hope for divine intervention and forces her into a debate about her religious convictions. When she suddenly faints, he finally begins to question whether he has any right to impose his ideas upon her; yet at the same time,

5: WHEAT AND POTATOES

he worries that his child will be influenced by its mother's religious misconceptions. He thinks the main elements of her belief are fear and superstition, and he feels compelled to help her overcome them.

Their religious disputes seem unavoidable. Susie wants to invite Father Williams to bless their livestock; the idea sounds so outlandish to Peder that he initially fails to understand it and later bursts into laughter. Predictably, Susie is offended by his reaction, but Peder has lost all patience with what he regards as her religious delusions.

The new Lutheran pastor of the settlement, Pastor Kaldahl, is a serious, taciturn man, who speaks little English. Beret invites him to a party during the Christmas season, where he lectures about Norwegian customs and history. He compares the great deeds of the best of their ancestors with the complacency of their contemporaries, worrying that mediocrity has become dominant in Norwegian America. He refutes the notion that America has a claim to being the land of the free before other lands, calling this view a piece of romantic nonsense. Scandinavia is the homeland of democracy, and Iceland is the world's oldest republic. How do the Norwegian-Americans take care of this heritage, however? They are ashamed of it and ape strange customs.

"A people that has lost its traditions is doomed," intones the pastor. When Peder voices his opposition by asserting that they are Americans, Kaldahl replies that a leopard does not lose his spots when he moves to new grounds and adds that it would not be in anyone's interest if they gave up their heritage. The Jews have preserved their identity over the centuries and contributed immensely to world civilization. In the United States, they are citizens as good as any—without forswearing their traditions. In contrast to Peder, Beret is so impressed with the new pastor that she donates ten dollars to the mission.

A few days later, while Peder and Susie are out one night, Beret falls down and injures herself. She is too old to recover. She asks Peder to teach his son Norwegian after she is gone and confesses to the pastor that she has had little Pete baptized by Sørine. Beret wants Susie to forgive her for having interfered with a mother's rights, but the latter leaves the room in disgust. After her mother-in-law's death, Susie expects a wake to be held and is terrified of sleeping in the same house with an unguarded dead body. During the night, she imagines seeing Beret's spirit and seeks help from Peder, but he only pushes her away. That night Susie loses the child she is carrying.

Peder realizes that many of his mother's warnings and prophecies have come true. "We do not keep wheat and potatoes in the same bin," she had said, and more and more he begins to understand what she had meant. In Nikoline, Sørine's niece who is visiting from northern Norway, Peder recognizes something he has not encountered before. Her appearance, her ways, and perhaps most of all her dialect strike a new cord within him. He enjoys her company and wishes he had met her before, but he knows that he must let her return to Norway.

At home, on the other hand, there is no end to the disagreements. Susie's devoutness is intensified by her ailment; she attends church frequently and perplexes Peder by being ash covered on Ash Wednesday. When he ridicules her again, she complains about his insensitivity toward other people's customs. Peder, for his part, has begun to read *Skandinaven,* a Norwegian-American newspaper, and has hired a Norwegian to help in the house.

Events move toward a final decision. Peder decides to run for county commissioner on the Republican ticket against Tom McDougal, an Irishman. The Dohenys and Father Williams support McDougal, and Susie behaves intransigently. When his opponent holds a rally whose purpose is the examination of Peder's character, Susie attempts to keep her husband from attending because she is aware of the content of McDougal's speech. Peder goes there anyway and witnesses how his opponent slanders him. McDougal, among other things, attacks his Lutheranism and his lack of religious devotion in general. He alludes to Beret's temporary insanity, holds Peder responsible for not having baptized his child, and accuses him of having kept his mother as a prisoner before she died. He then mentions that the child has finally been taken to baptism by its mother.

Senseless with rage, Peder barely manages to leave the meeting without physically assaulting McDougal. At home, Susie is aware of the state of events. When Peder arrives at the farm, she pretends that Pete is sick and tells Peder to go for a doctor, but he does not listen to her. She runs into her room and closes the door, but after a little while Peder walks in. One after the other, he destroys first the crucifix, then the font, and finally the rosary, calling this an end to the idolatry in their house.

When Peder wakes up the next morning, Susie has left with the child. She will never come back.

* * *

In the two last volumes of his Norwegian immigrant trilogy, Ole Edvart Rølvaag portrays the coming of age of the first generation that was born and raised in the new country. These Norwegian-Americans face a task very different from the one that confronted their parents. Instead of the overwhelming solitude of the untamed prairie, they encounter the omnipresence of the majority culture—a problem rarely experienced by the early settlers in these rural surroundings. The pioneers built their own structures, influenced by their natural and human environment, but essentially on their own terms. They had lived through their formative years in Norway; their cultural identity was established before they arrived in the new country. During the initial settlement period, little influence was exerted by the non-Norwegian establishment, whose cultural authority hardly reached the newly-won lands on the frontier.

All these factors are different for the children of the immigrants. They have grown up in America; Norway represents to them a land of tales and other people's reminiscences. Peder Holm speaks Norwegian with his mother, but the more time he spends away from the farm, the more the English language becomes his means of expression. Rølvaag exemplifies this split identity in the description of Peder's three symbolic rooms. In the first room, everything takes place in English. This is the room of the American reality, of the pioneer spirit, and of career expectations. In the second room, everything takes place in Norwegian. This is the room of his intimate family, particularly his mother. The third room is reserved for him and God—an uneasy relationship after God has taken his father away from him.

How does Rølvaag further his personal views about the preservation of ethnic characteristics in the novels? His characters are much more complex and less one-dimensional than are, for example, Simon Johnson's. There are no dark villains or shining knights.

Per Hansa dies before the onset of the ethnic struggle. Having transplanted Beret and thereby foreordaining his premature death, he does not live to see the consequences of his migration. His story is the story of the pioneer, in many ways the American story. Per Hansa is Norwegian only in the sense that he conforms with attitudes considered typical of northern European groups colonizing the American West; comparisons between the Scandinavian colonization of Iceland and settlement on the American prairie have been fairly popular. Whereas Per Hansa personifies the American immigrant, realizing one of many American dreams, his wife Beret forever remains the Norwegian emigrant, whose long life stretches to a point in time at which she sees her children turn into mainstream Americans.

Peder Seier is the novel's apparent protagonist. He expresses attitudes and opinions held by many second-generation Americans.

Rølvaag, the author, refrains from participating in the discussion, demonstrating a more advanced level of stylistic refinement than many other Norwegian-American writers. Peder clearly is drawn as a positive figure, and his views are presented without comment. The author seemingly gives his arguments a chance by letting them be put to the ultimate test—real life.

Peder does not think in ethnic and religious categories. He believes in the brotherhood of all Americans, regardless of their background. Consequently, he cannot understand why his mother tries to keep him away from the Irish. When he visits the Doheny family, he notices differences in the way they keep their house, but he attributes no further importance to them, rationalizing that lifestyles vary among Norwegians as well. The concept of a different faith fails to evoke strong emotions in him at first, since he has lost much of his childhood belief by the time he meets Susie Doheny.

Whereas abstract issues of ethnicity and religion initially remain on a philosophical level, the linguistic circumstances create practical discomforts for Peder. He desires nothing more than to be a normal American—and that means to be English speaking. The language on the farm is Norwegian, however, and Beret fights desperately against the overwhelming societal influences that estrange her son from his mother's tongue.

Peder follows his own ideas. He opposes his mother's attempts to preserve a Norwegian environment for her family, he marries an Irish girl, and a Catholic priest administers the wedding. The crossing of both ethnic and religious lines marks the complete realization of another American dream that lacks universal validity: the melting pot. Neither old-stock Americans nor immigrants gladly sacrificed their identity in order to be blended into a new one. On the contrary, they frequently nourished hopes of perpetuating their kind even under these new circumstances. Rølvaag puts this powerful American idea to the test. With *Paa veien til smeltepotten,* his friend Waldemar Ager devoted a complete novel to the refutation of the melting pot idea, which he and Rølvaag define as the complete amalgamation of the diverse ethnic and racial strains present in the United States into a new human specimen: the American. Rølvaag does not want to contribute to the endless theoretical dispute, which has followed him throughout his adult life. Instead, he tries to dispense with the melting pot as either a wonderful idea or a nightmare—it simply cannot be materialized. If not even someone as Americanized as Peder can live by its expectations, no one can.

5: WHEAT AND POTATOES

The remarkable development in the marriage between Peder and Susie is the resurgence of ethnic awareness. So much that has been taken for granted and has been viewed as natural behavior inherent to all mankind actually proves to be culture coded and alien to other people. The exposure to foreign ways of thinking and living, in turn, does not further understanding and relativism, but leads to a stronger emphasis on one's own traditions.

This reaction is not particularly new to social sciencists. People who experience "otherness" and the vulnerability of their own ways frequently become more aware, appreciative, and protective of the latter. The idea of tearing down borders often fails to resonate among the people living near these borders, since they know the way of life on both sides and are aware of the differences.

Peder's failure to live up to his professed openness contributes significantly to the tensions in his marriage. He tries to show understanding for Susie's traditions, but particularly in religious matters, he possesses little tolerance. As he repeatedly pokes fun at things that are dear to her, one cannot but notice his disregard for Catholicism, which he views as tainted with medieval superstition. Susie holds prejudiced opinions about Protestants, but she generally utters them only when she has to defend herself against Peder's attacks.

Behind both young people always loom the respective forces of tradition. Father Williams never truly accepts that a dear member of his flock has strayed so far. He expects Peder to further and encourage his wife's Catholic faith—an unrealistic demand to make of a man who has problems with merely tolerating this faith. Michael Doheny regrets having lost his capable daughter. Pastor Kaldahl reminds Peder of his obligations to his own people in America. Beret tries to raise little Pete as a Norwegian.

Pete becomes a pivotal point in this ongoing struggle. When Peder and Susie cannot agree on his religious upbringing, the baptism is delayed, but secretly both Beret and Susie have him baptized in their respective faiths. Michael Doheny never fails to detect Irish characteristics in the child; Beret sings Norwegian lullabies to him.

The endless arguments wear both spouses down. Susie enjoys the cozy familiarity of her father's house and is in no hurry to return to Beret's Norwegian farm. Peder experiences how Nikoline, the visitor from Norway, touches a place in his heart that no American has been able to touch before. The end comes as no surprise. Beret's death dramatically brings to light all the differences that have been present for a long time, and both spouses find their ultimate loyalties on their respective sides of the fence.

Quod erat demonstrandum. Rølvaag made his case quite convincingly, formulating his convictions without having to preach too much. He had faced a difficult task in the sequels to *Giants in the Earth*. The introductory novel was a song of praise for the accomplishments of the Norwegian pioneers. The conclusion of the trilogy, however, represented a contribution to a discussion that was of preeminent importance to Rølvaag. Its purpose went beyond art, and it is very difficult not to overburden the artistic framework with a message that is burning in one's heart. If Rølvaag largely succeeded in avoiding this problem, he accomplished more than did many others.

6
Preservationist Ideas in Fiction and in Political Discourse

THIS CHAPTER ANALYZES THE MAJOR IDEAS AND ARGUMENTS contained in the novels examined and puts them into their cultural and political context. In particular, literary are compared with nonliterary texts on the same subject. This comparison allows an examination of the ideological continuum present in the authors' texts and of its representation on different levels of discourse. Originally, only texts of the same author were meant to be compared, but it soon proved unnecessary to restrict the examination in this manner. The authors were part of the same intellectual movement; they participated in the same debate, encountered the same resistance, and faced the same realities. Therefore, arguments repeat themselves in the writings of other authors, allowing a tighter web of comparison. This recurrence of propositions also bestows historical credibility on the descriptions and reasonings presented in the texts: they clearly represent reality as seen by a particular group of Norwegian-Americans. The crisscross pattern of analysis may occasionally result in a repeated presentation of specific passages, but it allows a more exact extraction of the ideological content.

The nonfiction material used in this chapter consists predominantly of articles written by Waldemar Ager and Ole Edvart Rølvaag, both of whom participated extensively in the political debate of the time. Less material by Simon Johnson and Hans Rønnevik was available—it is largely restricted to private letters. As indicated before, however, the commonality of basic sentiment among the authors balances the uneven source distribution. The fact that one can find that arguments forwarded by Ager in his newspaper recur in a novel by Rønnevik demonstrates that they were based on a shared worldview and represented authentic contemporary viewpoints.

It is important to remember the subjective perspective of the material presented here. The observation that certain fictional events or developments are confirmed by corresponding descriptions in other novels does not transform them into actual historical events. At the very least, however, they tell us something about the way of thinking that produced this literature and about the importance ascribed to individual issues, since the extent of the analysis essentially mirrors the availability of source material.

The Language Question

The Norwegian language was viewed as the single most important element of Norwegian ethnicity, and its preservation among the immigrants and their offspring presented itself as a vital task. Norwegian is the language of their kin, of their ancestors, reminds Rølvaag, who always preserved a deep affection for his mother, who had stayed behind in Norway.[1] He laments in a speech delivered on Norwegian Constitution Day in 1907 that his fellow immigrants too often think that it is "much more stylish to stammer in broken English than to use their own rich and sonorous dialect."[2] One can find similar attitudes in Ager's *Paa veien til smeltepotten*. Here Lars dreams about returning to Norway with an American wife, impressing everyone by conversing elegantly in English. In reality, Lars' dream conversation is taking place in his faulty immigrant language.[3]

Lars is not the only one whose actual command of the English language is not commensurate with his pretenses. Mrs. Dale's daughter Gertie, who works as a servant girl in a nearby town, writes to her mother in English, even though the latter cannot read this language. Far from being taken aback by this circumstance, Mrs. Dale publicly admires her daughter for being able to write in English and for having forgotten every last word of Norwegian. Neither she nor her immigrant friends realize how poor and full of Norwegianisms is the language in Gertie's letter.

Henry Nelson's Norwegian-born mother harbors similar sentiments. She has barely been able to communicate with her son throughout his school years because they lacked a common language. When Henry temporarily finds himself in a Scandinavian working-class environment, his command of Norwegian expands rapidly, and he is finally able to converse freely with his mother. Mrs. Nelson, however, dislikes this development. She does not want a Norwegian immigrant for a son. She dreams about an American, even if this American son has nothing in common with her.[4]

Ultimately, the immigrant who surrenders his family to the forces of Americanization becomes an outsider who no longer feels at home in his own house. Thore Overhus exemplifies this development. If he speaks Norwegian, his family reacts with indignation; if he addresses them in English, they correct his mistakes. Even his youngest son, a little boy, rectifies his father's faulty English.[5] There seems to be no use for Norwegian for anyone aspiring to move ahead in the new country; Norwegian is reserved for those at the bottom of the ladder. Therefore, Mrs. Overhus, who rarely speaks Norwegian otherwise, always uses this language around Lars in order to remind him of his newcomer status.

In addition to depicting these practical inconveniences of precipitate language change, the authors also advance more idealistic arguments. To Ager, it would be tantamount to decay for a people to give up its language.[6] His views, put in religious terms, are echoed by the fictional Beret in Rølvaag's novel. As Ager asserts that "one would think that the mother tongue would be as sacred and inviolable to us as it is to the Danes and Poles living in Germany,"[7] Beret tells the pastor that she considers it sinful that he spoke English in her home, because it surely must be a sin to disregard one's mother tongue.[8]

Having maintained that it is necessary to preserve the ancestral language in the new country, the writers also argue that it is feasible. Ager and Rølvaag both advocate the teaching of Norwegian as a subject at Midwestern schools. In order to counter the argument that the younger generation lacks the interest level necessary for preserving the mother tongue, Ager creates desirable usages in his novel. A temperance lodge serves as a catalyst for reviving the Norwegian language among young people, similar to the youth club in Rønnevik's *100 procent*. Both exemplify the creation of social clubs for second-generation Norwegian-Americans, where they can socialize with each other and retain their culture in an informal and effortless manner. Clearly, the enthusiastic descriptions are meant to instigate a desire for imitation.

Where should the children receive their initial instruction in Norwegian? Rølvaag's response to this question illustrates the difficulties involved. Peder Holm speaks Norwegian with his mother, but when she attempts to have him read aloud from the Bible, he resists. It does not come naturally for him; he has to be coaxed into it, and the element of compulsion undermines the success because it interferes with a positive attitude toward the language.[9]

The most common place for children to encounter written Norwegian at that time was in church. Sunday school and confirmation instruction were frequently held in this language. Rølvaag points out the problems:

> It is surprising how much Norwegian some of the brightest children have acquired this way. One thing was missing nevertheless: love. And in many cases it became neither fish nor fowl, neither Norwegian language nor religion. It must also have happened that children started to loathe both in this manner. The long and difficult words, and even more so the abstract concepts in the Catechism strangled the interest in the language. We did not even bother to put these study books into modern, natural language. Both the spelling and the idioms are based on the Danish that was used in Norway around the middle of the last century.[10]

In *Paa veien til smeltepotten,* the words are almost the same:

> His childhood had been overshadowed by the Norwegian parochial school. At his house they only spoke English; but his father, who was a very serious Lutheran of the old school, had demanded that he should attend the Norwegian parochial school and learn his catechism in Norwegian. And he had crammed it in the shadow of the rod. First, it was the Ten Commandments and the rod. Then it was the articles of the Apostles' Creed or the rod and the Lord's Prayer and the rod or the threat of the rod. He had sat and chewed on long words such as *nidkjærhed* (zeal), *vederkvægelse* (comfort), *retfærdiggjørelse* (absolution) and *vederstyggelighed* (abomination) until they gyrated within him and almost made him nauseous.[11]

In spite of these deplorable conditions, the Norwegian parochial schools were ascribed a significant cultural role. Ager has the moribund Omley request Norwegian religious instruction for his son, so that he would forget neither his father nor his creator. The problematic implications of almost complete reliance on religious institutions for the preservation of Norwegian ethnic traditions emerge most visibly in the teaching practice at Norwegian language schools, where the language is clearly subservient to theological goals and suffers accordingly.

As a college teacher of Norwegian, Rølvaag is constantly concerned with ways of preserving the immigrant language. He implores the parents to create a Norwegian environment for their children by always speaking this language at home and by providing them with Norwegian books appropriate for their age. Ager points out that everything else would have been achieved in vain if the children will not learn Norwegian—they will lose interest in their heritage, and the cultural values brought along by the immigrants will disappear. It seems peculiar that no successful application of these suggestions appears in any of the novels, which show an almost universal decline in the use of the ancestral language among the second generation, very much in agreement with reality. The desire to create literature with a basis in fact apparently prevented the authors from transferring all of their political demands into their novels. Such realism also indicates the limited echo the preservationist suggestions received in the immigrant population.

Judging by the novels, a different situation was much more common. The isolated pioneer who is shoved aside because he or she cannot communicate in English equally well as the younger generation recurs in several descriptions. Mrs. Skare does not share a common language with her children in *Paa veien til smeltepotten* and turns into a domestic robot in her family's eyes. When Lovise, in *Frihetens hjem,* points out that old people need the Church's consolation in their mother tongue, Ager's novel supplies a practical example of this need. After he was called to the dying Mrs. Nelson, the pastor reads for her in halting and flawed Norwegian, and the author makes sure that the message is not missed by the reader:

> He could not possibly have a dictionary at hand when he knelt by the sickbed and was very much excused for that. He was also sure that God excused him; but Karoline did not excuse him, and when he had left she read to the sick woman.[12]

The most important question in this debate concerned the possibility of survival for the Norwegian language in an American environment. Rølvaag considers this point so crucial that he uses the heavy-handed device of direct author intervention to bring his message across:

> And the younger ones needed English; the young generation would have to defend its faith in the country's language. In 20 years one would not hear one word of Norwegian in America!—This prediction took root. When the language question was tearing apart congregations 25 years later, it surfaced again and became a slogan.[13]

Here Rølvaag creates his own historical argument for use in the contemporary discussion. By having his fictional pastor make the same predictions about the Norwegian language's imminent demise with which his own opponents confront him decades later, he proves them wrong—at least in the world of his novels. The significance Rølvaag ascribes to this particular argument can be seen by his resort to direct author intervention, which rarely occurs in his novels.

Personal and Topographical Names

Names might appear to be of marginal importance compared to a truly central issue such as language use, but they contain a symbolic value. Both personal and place names indicate the presence of a particular group in the area; they stake a claim to the land. The preservationist viewpoint with regard to personal names can easily be detected in the names Rølvaag and Ager gave their own children. Rølvaag's children were baptized Ella Valborg, Karl Fridtjof, Paul Gunnar, and Olaf Arnljot. Ager named his children Trygve, Magne, Solveig, Valborg, Roald, Eyvind, Gudrun, Hildur, and Borghild.

Beret clearly shares the views of her literary creator. When her first grandchild is called Henry Percival, she perceives this name as an insult to his Norwegian heritage. In her anger, she stays away from him at first, even though she closely follows his development from a distance. When her second grandson is baptized Randolph Osborne, she bears this cross with silent resignation. Rølvaag also supplies a reassuring example of the viability of Norwegian names and has Else, the pastor's daughter, praise Peder's middle name Seier.

Rønnevik's role models prefer Norwegian names. Guri Brenden bestows them upon all her sons, and Louis Olson even reassumes his grandfather's name, Lars Holte. This unusual event stands in direct contrast to the more common name change from Lars to Louis Olson in *Paa veien til smeltepotten*. Both incidents are described for the same purpose, however, because Lars Holte functions as a positive example, whereas the newcomer Louis Olson represents the assimilationist social climber who surrenders his most valuable attributes to succeed within American society.

Johnson supplies negative examples of name change as well. Whereas Jerome Audobon Mostead at least received his name from his parents, who were born as Norwegian Mostads, Matias Mastlie assumes the grandiose Marx Glibb Masterley of his own choosing.

Johnson also portrays involuntary Anglicization by native-born Americans, who regularly alter Braastad to Braystead regardless of the family's personal preferences.

World War I brought about a sharp decline in everything "foreign," including names. *100 procent* contains examples of how the names of businesses and topographic features were changed during that time period. Pete Harmsen quietly drops the word *Scandinavian* from the name of his bank, whereas the replacement of "Bismarck Avenue" by "Washington Avenue" is accompanied by anti-German mob scenes. These examples, more than anything else, demonstrate the symbolic significance contained in names—a significance that did not go unnoticed by ethnic intellectuals.

Education

No other institution exerted more influence on the fortunes of Norwegian cultural life in the New World than the school. From the moment they had reached school age, the children slipped away from their parents' control and entered a new world. In pretelevision rural America, school represented the first significant outside influence on the immigrant child. Today, most children cannot be sheltered from the majority culture even before they reach school age, but in the relative isolation of the pioneer Midwest, parental cultural habits remained largely unchallenged until school started.

The immigrant authors feared the assimilatory influence of the American education system. Rølvaag maintains that the common school leads the children away from their parents and cuts the tie between the child and its home.[14] In *Peder Seier,* he describes this development in literary form. Miss Mahon, the Yankee teacher, scolds the Norwegian children for speaking with an accent. She advises Peder to use only English at home in order to eliminate interferences from Norwegian and embarrasses him by pointing out his mother's limited command of the country's language. The children receive no information about the land of their ancestors—a picture of Norway in one of his schoolbooks is the full extent of what Peder learns about this country. As a consequence of his school attendance, Peder increasingly switches to English as his main language, restricting Norwegian largely to communication with his mother.

Not only the public schools lead the children away from their parents' culture. According to Rølvaag, the situation in Norwegian-Lutheran parochial schools is little different:

> No, many of our schools are not Norwegian-American institutions; they are American, and some even are so ultra-American that they are hostile toward everything Norwegian.[15]

Tallaksa school in *Peder Seier* represents such an institution. Although all the students come from Norwegian homes, the blackboard reads that this is an American school where only English is to be spoken. Rølvaag has to concede, however, that outside pressure is not solely responsible for the estrangement of young people from their ancestral language. His own experience at St. Olaf College demonstrated to him that many students tried to avoid taking Norwegian. Rølvaag does not want them to have a choice in that matter—Norwegian should be obligatory for Norwegian-American students, and high schools in Norwegian settlement areas should offer it.[16] Instead of studying Spanish or German, the students would gain access to their own cultural background. The combined disinterest of both the students and the majority society explains why Rølvaag's suggestions were rarely put into practice.

CHURCH

Next to the schools, the churches were the most significant cultural institutions in immigrant life. In the case of the Norwegians, Church essentially meant one of a number of Norwegian-Lutheran denominations. These religious communities were founded by and for immigrants, but eventually they, too, felt the acculturation process that was taking place. As they were the primary supporters of Norwegian institutions in the new country, the language debate raged more violently within them than almost anywhere else. The preservationist authors all referred to aspects of this debate in their works.

During the pioneer days, the Church had preserved home-country traditions. Ager consequently defended it against the famous Norwegian author Bjørnstjerne Bjørnson, who had criticized it during his tour through North America:

> Bjørnstjerne Bjørnson was probably the most prominent Norwegian to visit us. No one is a more passionate Norwegian than he is. But in his

speeches he chose to attack the Church, which has proven to be the strongest Norwegian power among us and which has saved ten times more of our ancestral heritage than all other cultural powers put together.[17]

This positive cultural role of the Church finds an echo in the novels, predominantly in reference to the original settlement period. In *100 procent*, the retired pastor disapproves of his successor's anti-Norwegian stance, and in *Frihetens hjem*, the old pastor Bry is assailed during World War I for using Norwegian in church. More often, however, one encounters a younger pastor who views the Norwegian language as a liability for the Lutheran Church and actively works toward its complete replacement by English. Rønnevik's Pastor Johnson, who exploits the antiforeign atmosphere of the war years to increase the role of English in his congregation and cooperates with the Anglo-American elite in his district, exemplifies this type of clergyman. Also, Rølvaag's Pastor Gabrielsen and Ager's pastor see no future for Norwegian in either church or country. Gabrielsen generally uses English when dealing with young people, and he provides Peder with an English Bible in order to prepare him for the English-speaking future. These assimilationist ministers regard the Anglicization of the Church as necessary for its survival. Ager disagrees with this view:

> The immigrants will not feel at home in congregations in which the sermon is in English, in which the youth clubs use English, and in which the assembly is often held in the same language. There are no studies to refer to; yet the author has gotten the impression that newcomers who speak a little English prefer all-American churches to those that are part the one and part the other.[18]

In the novel, he elaborates on this view. The newcomer Lars feels isolated in the visibly Anglicized local Norwegian-Lutheran church, whose pastor wants to abolish all Norwegian services, even though the increased role of English has failed to make the congregation more attractive to the younger generation. At the same time, the church loses potential new members:

> But the day could not be far off when everything had to be in English. He was concerned, however, about the decrease in church attendance. The newcomers went to a different congregation where Norwegian was used exclusively. He heard that church attendance there had increased.[19]

These newcomers should be the Church's prime source of new members according to Rølvaag, who ascribes a religious disposition to the Norwegian people and foresees them as the future flag bearers for Christianity. He admonishes his Church that its foremost duty lies with its own, the Norwegian people.

When the assimilationists pointed to the needs of the future as represented by the widely Americanized younger generation, the preservationists retorted by underlining the Church's responsibility to its older members, upon whose sacrifices the Church was built. In *100 procent,* the widow Gundhild leaves the congregation in despair when the Norwegian services are discontinued. She had never learned English, but, together with her husband, she had helped build the church. Now she feels as isolated as the moribund immigrants in *Paa veien til smeltepotten,* who silently beg the pastor for the Norwegian Bible. Not wanting to be reminded that English does not reach everyone in his congregation, the pastor feels uncomfortable during such incidents.

Occasionally, the authors try to establish the viability of Norwegian as a means of communicating with the younger generation. Rønnevik has the retired pastor participate actively in a Norwegian youth club, and Rølvaag's description of a similar association sounds like an encouragement to copy this wonderful idea. Rølvaag also portrays the congregation's bewilderment when first confronted with confirmations in English. Generally, even preservationists must acknowledge, however, that the Church's language policy is responding to the mood among its younger members. During the war, there are additional outside pressures—as witnessed in *Frihetens hjem* by the attacks on Pastor Bry, who is assailed for speaking Norwegian and teaching German theology—but to a large extent the demand for Anglification originates within the Church.

In addition to the language debate within the Norwegian-Lutheran Church, other religious issues are delineated, but none in such a universal and detailed manner. Rølvaag spends much time on the doctrinal conflicts between the Lutheran Beret Holm, her son Peder, who has lost much of his childhood faith, and his Catholic wife Susie. The increasing bitterness of these disputes is undoubtedly meant to serve as a warning against interfaith and interethnic marriages. Due to the dearth of comparable fiction or nonfiction material, this question cannot easily be put into a sensible context. It suffices to indicate here that Rølvaag clearly developed this topic along ideologically predetermined lines.

The broad space allotted to religious matters in the writings of these authors—none of whom was a pastor himself—indicates their importance in contemporary Norwegian-American society. The immigrants brought along their Lutheran Church, which contained memories of a long history—a history that the pioneer generation did not want to relinquish. The high level of historical accuracy achieved in the literary descriptions becomes obvious upon comparison with an official Church view:

> There have been pastors who have lived and worked in this country year after year and who have downright made an honor of the shameful fact that they have no command of the country's language. . . .
> But there are not many of them left. The tide has turned. The advancement of English is moving ahead so quickly that it is hardly necessary now to speed it up. At some places it goes so fast that the older ones, who have built both the congregation and the church building, feel pushed out of both. There are places where the treatment of the old "Norwegians" is downright tragic. Not long ago, we listened to reports of this kind in our office; they were told by reliable and trusting people; tearful eyes gave evidence of how strongly the person felt about his new position in the Church. . . .[20]

INTERGENERATIONAL RELATIONS

Nowhere does cultural change touch the immigrants closer to home than through their children. Whereas they themselves will forever remain shaped by their upbringing in the old country, their children will undergo their socialization process in the new environment. Consequently, assimilation will often make its first inroads into the home through the children, and the customary intergenerational strife will acquire a cultural overtone. These differences can revolve around an obviously ethnic trait such as language, but also around less manifestly cultural behavioral patterns.

Waldemar Ager explores the intergenerational relationship in the immigrant family both in literary and in nonliterary form. His verdict on the second generation is frequently negative, because in his eyes the American-born children of Norwegian immigrants do not accomplish nearly as much as could be expected of them. In spite of having the advantage of growing up within the new culture, the young generation brings forth fewer societal success stories than their parents'.[21] In *Paa veien til smeltepotten*, Ager elaborates on this view. He describes how young newcomers quickly find jobs and work their way up, whereas the high school graduates of the second generation pass time aimlessly, waiting for a position that fits them. The young sons of the Omleys already display this tendency toward idleness in their childhood, spending hours playing ball, as native American boys do, without feeling the slightest desire to help at home. Young American-born women receive a similarly unflattering description. Ager views them as an expensive financial liability,[22] and the newly-arrived Karoline in Ager's novel perceives them as spoiled and shallow.

Ager detects a feeling of superiority in the young, Americanized generations. They look down on their immigrant parents, even though they depend on their financial support, and the parents secretly concede their inferiority because the children have achieved what has remained elusive to them—to act and sound like a native:

> The children therefore felt linguistically superior to their parents. The parents had nothing to tell their children to make them feel attached to them, and they could not help them with their homework. The parents' "Americanness" was not painted on thick enough for the children not to discover the "old-country traits", which the parents themselves despised, under it. They learned to look down on them.[23]

In another article, Ager refers to personal experiences when he writes:

> The women want "smart" children, and they tell each other proudly that their children do not understand a single word of Norwegian. Not a word—if they want to be really swank. What the women themselves can say is restricted to household words such as "Shut your mouth", "Quit that monkey business", and the like. Then comes the day—a bitter day—when the parents discover that they cannot converse intelligently with their own children.[24]

Paa veien til smeltepotten provides almost the identical portrayal:

> *Jeg vi'kke ta no'n Monkeybisnis a dig, Sophy. Hurry up kvik nu med en Gang* . . . Mrs. Omley could never remain angry long enough to finish a longer sentence. And when Sophy became angry and spoke English, there was something so elegant and ladylike about her daughter that she often became embarrassed at the thought of her own simpleness.[25]

Berntine Nelson is another mother who is in awe of her son—with whom she can hardly communicate. When this son temporarily accepts a job as a manual laborer and learns passable Norwegian, his mother is deeply dismayed; she only regains her happiness when he finds a wealthy American wife. One of her friends, all of whom are immigrant women, suggests that Berntine would be better off if her son had married a simple girl who could relate to her. Mrs. Nelson vehemently disagrees—the son lives the life the immigrant mother dreams about, and she participates vicariously in his apparent success. The children, on the other hand, frequently try to hide their parents from their American friends. Outsiders are only shown the stately family portraits on the wall, not the parents themselves, who become little more than providers and servants because their children surpass them at the most precious characteristic for the assimilation-minded immigrant—an inconspicuous American identity.

The Political Sphere

All four novels were written during the first decades of the twentieth century; two of them portray contemporary events. Rølvaag chooses an earlier setting because he wants to describe the original settlement period. Ager does not become involved with politics as such, as long as it does not directly concern the survival of Norwegian-American culture. The two remaining novels display many basic similarities, and the major part of their plots takes place during World War I. Contrasting their ideological message is highly informative because it demonstrates how divergent the views of preservationists can become as soon as the issue is not strictly tied to the ethnic question.

When Peder Holm runs for office on the Republican ticket, the opposing Populists are described negatively, but not in detail. Rølvaag does not want to dwell on this issue. Simon Johnson's dislike for the agrarian protest movement, on the other hand, is clearly visible in his writings. In tune with the author's general disposition toward black and white depiction, some of the leading assimilationists in his novel also work for the Populist Nonpartisan League. Johnson portrays the movement as demagogic and extremist and accuses it of detracting the farmers from cultural issues. His earlier collection of short stories, *Fire fortællinger* (Four Short Stories), had already abounded with negative references to Populist politics. Johnson's tendency toward ideological oversimplification becomes most tangible in his treatment of the war years, because in tune with Johnson's own preferences, the protagonist Olaf Nelson is in favor of Norwegian culture and the war, whereas his opponents represent an unlikely coalition of such diverse groups as American nativists and Norwegian-American opponents of the war.

Whereas Rølvaag and especially Johnson express opposition to the Midwestern farm movement, Rønnevik develops a more sympathetic picture. His leading character, Lars Holte, cannot actively support the movement either, but a number of exemplary Norwegians do. Rønnevik's representation of the war debate and of the camps that formed sounds more convincing than Johnson's because his coalition of Yankee leaders and assimilated Norwegians appears plausible. They demand 100 percent—culturally and politically—and everyone who opposes the war or a monolingual American society becomes their enemy. Rønnevik also catches the spirit of the time when he portrays the violent measures taken against dissenters, such as effigy hangings and the disruption of political meetings. He uses authentic events for some of his scenes, depicting the prominent Midwestern senators La Follette and Gronna. While criticizing the enticing propaganda of the NPL, Rønnevik also illustrates the force applied against this party by its opponents inside and outside of government. Its rallies are prohibited by the sheriff, its speakers are tarred and feathered, and its local printing press is destroyed by hired thugs.

The prehistory of America's entry into the war is not in and of itself an element of the debate over ethnicity. In view of the fact that the public atmosphere created by the war also produced an intense Americanization drive, the portrayal of this development, nevertheless, deserves a brief investigation. Simon Johnson presents a straightforward, if somewhat simplistic, explanation of America's reasons for entering the war. Germany had ruthlessly mocked the United States for years. The Allies were not only the defenders of democracy but were also hopelessly outnumbered (a not necessarily convincing contention in view of the distinct numerical superiority of the Entente). Therefore, Johnson views America's entry into the war as a glorious act of selfless sacrifice. He faced the delicate problem, however, that the very circles that agitated most fervently in favor of American intervention also demanded the immediate assimilation of all immigrant groups. In order to preserve his model of good and evil, Johnson had to create a protagonist who, like Johnson himself, combined a pro-Norwegian with a prowar stance. This could still be done credibly, particularly because the protagonist Olaf Nelson only gradually moves toward supporting a military intervention. The character development of his assimilationist opponents, who are depicted as only pretending to support the war, appears less convincing. One would expect a larger number of them to view the political situation the way Johnson himself did, but the author could not tolerate the idea that the opponents of Norwegian culture might be exonerated by their American patriotism.

Rønnevik approaches this problem more convincingly because he is more in tune with the Midwestern sentiment of the era. He describes how the general Midwestern populace sees no reason for participating in a war that does not concern them. In contrast to other parts of the country, neither emotional bonds with Britain nor economic interests influence them in favor of the Allies. The press and most other institutions of power intimidate opponents of the war and try to set the population against Germany by disseminating less than reliable reports of German wartime conduct. In Rønnevik's depiction, the interventionists also undermine immigrant culture in the name of 100 percent Americanism.

Johnson shares the anti-German sentiments of the nativists to the point of expressing his objections to American intolerance by assailing it as an example of the German spirit. Rønnevik, on the other hand, openly rejects the wartime rhetoric; similarly, he displays a sympathetic understanding for the difficult role in which German-Americans suddenly find themselves.

The political differences between Johnson and Rønnevik mirror the diametrically opposed role of the two Norwegian-American senators of that time. Knute Nelson, the conservative senator from Minnesota, denounced the agrarian protest movement and actively supported America's intervention in Europe. Asle Gronna, on the other hand, the Populist senator from North Dakota who plays a significant role in *100 procent,* was one of merely six senators who voted against the American declaration of war. In spite of intense pressure, only four of the ten Norwegian-Americans in Congress were in support of American intervention, which is an indication that Rønnevik's views were more common than Johnson's.[26] Still, the combined impressions collected from these novels render a fairly accurate picture of the debate within the Norwegian community.

The authors' conflicting viewpoints about America's societal elites make the ultimate outcome of the war experience noticeably different for Olaf Nelson and Lars Holte. Both are accused of unpatriotic behavior. Whereas a wise judge not only clears Olaf but actually praises him as an exemplary patriot, Lars is sent to jail. Rønnevik's disillusionment with the spirit of the time runs much deeper than Johnson's.

The Concept of Ethnicity

Much of what has been examined so far has been viewed in an ethnic context. This distinct heading "ethnicity" introduces an examination of the authors' contribution to the topic's more theoretical aspects. The analysis helps to establish the underlying *Weltanschauung* permeating the writings and their implicit understanding of Norwegian-American cultural development.

Ager divides the history of active Norwegian preservationism into three parts. At first the immigrants fenced themselves in. The Lutheran congregation formed the center of cultural activity, shielding against outside influences. Then, when the Church's interest in Norwegian ethnicity faded, the *bygdelag* movement started. These regional associations gathered people around popular, hometown traditions. They did not stress esoteric subjects such as the dramas by Henrik Ibsen or the history of the Vikings, but featured food and dances from the immigrants' home districts. This internal movement was followed by the Sons of Norway, a society consisting predominantly of American-born members. This last organization aims to represent Norwegian interests in the larger American society, based on a largely symbolic ethnicity among widely Americanized generations.

Ager distinguishes two forms of Americanization: Americanization of one's tongue and Americanization of one's life. Only the latter has relevance for the country, he says. Everyone who dedicates his life and his labor to the new country has become an American, no matter what language he speaks. Ager wants to overcome the inferiority complex among his fellow immigrants, assuring them that by creating immeasurable values through their cultivation of the wilderness, they have given more to the country than they have received. They do not owe America the additional sacrifice of forsaking their mother tongue.

Rønnevik has the Norwegian pioneer Thormod Kvinnesdal utter the same thoughts. Kvinnesdal refutes the notion that the settlers have to be thankful to America, arguing that the opposite is true. They created farmland for America, and America should thank them by allowing them to live according to their own traditions. Immigrants have every reason to be proud of who they are, but Ager claims that they try to hide their identity, living in constant fear of revealing themselves. In the novel, the Norwegian-American newcomer Lars Olson camouflages the Norwegian newspaper he is reading by placing it inside an American one, so passersby can only see the American paper. Even in their private eating habits they try to shed their "foreign" identity:

> They possibly adopt an English or American diet, but they have poor digestion and receive most pleasure from their table implements and the names of dishes.[27]

In *Paa veien til smeltepotten,* the situation is depicted the same way:

> ... so she started on a "boiled dinner". The ladies in the Presbyterian church had served one last winter, and it was reported in the papers. But she came to regret this decision later and was regretting it now. . . .[28]

Ager compares the assimilation process to a religious revival. First, immigrants must acknowledge their shame, namely, the misery of their former country. Then, they have to convert by cutting all ties to the past. Finally, they become sanctified by ignoring or hating everything that used to be dear to them and by loving only what the authorities prescribe. The basic sentiment expressed in this description permeates much of Ager's literary production.

Rølvaag introduces the figure of Pastor Kaldahl as a means of presenting theoretical viewpoints on ethnic identity. This pastor, who bears similarity with the real-life Norwegian-Lutheran pastor Kildahl, points to the significance of preserving one's heritage. "A people without tradition is doomed," he passionately admonishes Peder. When the latter insists that he is an American, Kaldahl retorts that a leopard does not change his spots when he moves to a new ground. He cites the Jews as an example of a people that has preserved its traditions while living among others. Kaldahl (as Rølvaag) desires a similar coexistence for the Norwegians in America.

Simon Johnson also elaborates on conceptual aspects of ethnicity. His protagonist Olaf Nelson explains that not only trees, but humans, too, are dependent on their most tender roots. He defines culture as finding the new while preserving everything good that has been collected through time. During his court trial, he accounts for his views and delineates that British and Irish immigrants cultivate their traditions without arousing suspicion. He expects America to grant its Norwegian citizens the same rights, and at least in the novel, American society, represented by the judge, concurs.

Philiopietistic arguments are used when Olaf Nelson, who traveled to Norway to discover his roots just as Simon Johnson did, writes to his fiancée Lovise about the greatness of their ancestors. He tells his sister-in-law that he has met someone who looks just like her, underlining the family ties between the continents. Old Braastad wonders if his son's life could not have been stabilized by being more strongly rooted in his heritage.

The preservationist authors stand in the tradition of European ethnic nationhood—most visibly in the works of Rølvaag and Ager. When Rølvaag has Beret declare that wheat and potatoes do not belong in the same bin, she speaks as an ethnic nationalist, as does Ager when he expresses his grief about the home country he has lost. Nowhere is this worldview expressed more clearly than at the point where Ager describes his emotions during a visit to Norway:

> We came to understand that our heart was not attached to rocks, to trees or the soil or similar things, but to our kin, to the people—*our* people. The greatest experience during a visit to Norway is to hear the children speak Norwegian in the streets and to know that they are all Norwegians here—the old ones, the young ones, the genteel ones, the simple ones—they are all our *own*.[29]

This observation reflects Ager's interest in underlying emotional correlations. Many emigrants might indeed think that it is the land they are missing but would be greatly disappointed if they found the places of their youth inhabited by a different people. Ager adds that Americans value the diversity of Europe, whereas they want to erase this diversity in their own country. The cultural identity of the various European peoples is seen as a precondition for their great intellectual and artistic achievements.[30]

Ager's relationship to his origins is deeply influenced by the emigrant experience. To many emigrants, Norway is something special—they regard every Norwegian as their brother, but native Norwegians do not always return this affection. Many Norwegian-Americans, moreover, remember a Norway that no longer exists, because they have not experienced the changes the country has gone through. All these factors contribute to the creation of a mythic home country, of a highly personal image of Norway.

Images of Norway and America

Most immigrants would not approach the ethnic question in an abstract manner. To them, Norway and the United States were two very concrete entities to which they had to relate. The images of these countries developed by the Norwegian-American authors often centered on the origins and the makeup of American identity. Ager observed that "American" too often means "British" and added that immigrants would be willing to melt into something completely new but do not want to sacrifice their own heritage in favor of someone else's.

America is seen as a young country that has not yet reached cultural maturity. Ager expounds that Wisconsin has not produced any great writers even though so many of its inhabitants came from very literary countries. Rølvaag agrees that Americans have not yet become a writing people; they are rootless and constantly looking for amusement. Only what pays has value. Americans are also described as spendthrifts, compared to the economical Norwegian immigrants. In *Frihetens hjem,* they look down on immigrants and demand their immediate and complete assimilation.

By presenting an idealized picture of old-stock New Englanders, the writers also allude to a very different kind of American. The strength of the contemporary image is evidenced by its appearance in both *Paa veien til smeltepotten* and *Frihetens hjem.* In the former novel, Lovise longs for the true American spirit, whose home lies in a mythical Northeast. This is the place where the real Americans live, as opposed to the Midwest, where half-assimilated immigrants and crude frontier-Americans oppress other cultures and make a mockery of their own. In Ager's novel, the immigrant Karoline finds work with Judge Highbee, who personifies a noble New England aristocracy that is quickly disappearing under the onslaught of the huddled masses. Rølvaag asserts that the Norwegians could become for the Northwest what the British have been for New England.[31]

Both Lars Holte and Olaf Nelson initially depict America as the promised land, but their divergent wartime experiences lead to different conclusions. In Johnson's and Rønnevik's descriptions, one finds recurrent themes with a diametrically opposed interpretation. Johnson supplies the following reasons for America's entry into the war:

> This was America—and America went to war without any hope for gains, this was America too, this was America's noble power, now the world would see the nation the way it was.... But the motive was not the expansion of its own power, but rather the sacrifice of power for the sake of others, and which other nation would do a thing like that?[32]

Rønnevik has heard the same arguments, but he reiterates them with undisguised irony:

> All things considered, this is a religious mission for us. America did not go to war for its own national gain. We are meant to save the world. And even these godless ones, the barbarians, will be allowed to live once we have thoroughly defeated them.[33]

In these and other passages, Rønnevik makes it clear how differently from Johnson he views America's role in World War I. The latter echoes the wartime argumentation, even though the book is written years later, whereas Rønnevik cannot hide his ironic detachment from the public ideology of this era. His protagonist, Lars Holte, had begun to question his feelings toward America before the war:

> America was a rich country.... The Lord must have been in a bright mood when he created it. And here should be abundance for everyone. Out here everything was distributed fairly evenly indeed. No one suffered privation. But in other places? ...
> Why were his relatives and fellow citizens astonished when he took back his old name? Had it already come to the point that people had lost a sense for things that marked the greatness of their lineage?[34]

He still professes his undivided loyalty to the United States, but his belief in the country is eroding. Meanwhile, Thormod Kvinnesdal, who was born in Norway, inspires him with his accounts of the cultural and historical accomplishments of their ancestors.

Ties to the old country can also express themselves through the transfer of Norwegian customs to America. An important institution in rural Norway was the *odalsrett*, which tied a farm to family and kin.[35] The United States, stressing individualism and mobility, had no room for such restrictions on the sovereignty of personal property, but three of the four authors aspire to a perpetuation of this rural Norwegian institution. Guri Brenden in *100 procent* views their homestead as an *odalsgård*, as does Jens Braastad in *Frihetens hjem*, and Beret Holm lays out the traditional restrictions on selling the farm outside the family in her will. The significance ascribed to this tradition reaches beyond the fact that it is Norwegian. The preservationists sensed the connection between a community-based way of life on a family level and on a nationality level. A society of tradition-bound family farmers would provide the most favorable conditions for the continuation of Norwegian ethnicity in the new environment.

Another important aspect of transatlantic connections is the mutual understanding between those who left Norway and those who stayed behind. Waldemar Ager wrote an entire article on this topic, in which he reveals his disappointment at those in Norway who fail to understand the love that is shown them by their emigrated conationals. There are petty frictions, such as the snobbishness toward America prevalent among the upper classes in Norway—and in Europe in general—and the bragging that frequently accompanies return visits of Norwegian-Americans. Yet Ager is more concerned about the lack of reciprocity he perceives in the emotional relationship between Norwegians in America and Norwegians in the old country.[36]

The immigrants not only have to relate to Norway and the Norwegians, but even more so to America and the Americans. They must defend themselves against suspicions of disloyalty for trying to preserve "foreign" traits and loyalties. In this debate, which intensified during World War I, the preservationists insist that there is no conflict between their cultural and their political loyalties. Rølvaag asserts that they even owe it to their new country to preserve their heritage:

> When Americans of Italian descent, of Russian descent, of British descent, of Norse descent, etc., have succeeded in perpetuating what is best in their respective races in the future nation and its civilization, then and only then shall we have fulfilled our duty toward our country.[37]

This line of argument recurs with all activist authors. Olaf Nelson in *Frihetens hjem* states that his interest in Norway does not stand in the way of his American patriotism. During his court trial, he testifies that the growth he experienced by studying his heritage has actually served the United States. In *100 procent*, Lars Holte insists that taking his grandfather's (Norwegian) name reflected supreme American values. One can sense the accusations of un-American behavior against which preservationists are defending themselves; they considered it necessary to argue that they only preserved their heritage in order to benefit their new country. The frequency of these assurances indicates how much a part of the political debate these novels were and reaffirms their value as a key to the ideas of the authors and their time.

The Relationship to Other Ethnic Groups

The four authors occasionally referred to other immigrant groups. Rølvaag made the relationship between the Norwegian Peder and the

Irish Susie a central point of his novel, but only a few nonliterary sources on his views about the Irish can be found. He did believe in the existence of national characteristics, though, and contrasted Norwegian shyness with Irish pushiness in one of his theoretical works.[38] In his trilogy, he elaborates on the differences between the two nationalities and describes the Irish as warmhearted but not as organized and dependable as the Norwegians. The disparate standards of cleanliness occupy a prominent place in Rølvaag's description. He also indicates that several distinguishing social characteristics tend to coincide, such as Irish and Catholic and Liberal versus Norwegian and Lutheran and Republican. These overlapping loyalties have led some critics to interpret the arguments between Peder and Susie as religious in nature. It appears to be a more convincing interpretation, however, that Rølvaag tried to illustrate the ethnic irreconcilability by pointing to religious factors, among others.

The Germans are the only other immigrant group that receives considerable attention. Because of the time period during which these novels were written, the references deal with Germans in Germany at least as often as with German immigrants in America, and the two groups are not always neatly separated. Again—as on the related war issue—the opinions among the Norwegian authors differ noticeably. Johnson frequently denounces "the German spirit" in his novel and indicates in his unpublished autobiography that he approves of the measures taken against German-Americans, whose behavior had, in his eyes, provoked the antiforeign agitation.[39] Whereas Johnson cannot identify with the primary targets of the loyalism crusade, Rønnevik sympathetically portrays the plight of German-American individuals during the war years and rejects the campaign against all things German. Ager, who uses a different time period for his novel, also refers positively to German immigrants, viewing them as similar to Scandinavians in background and qualifications. There are minor descriptions of other groups; all but Rølvaag's references to the Jews, who are presented as an example of a community that preserves its character while successfully participating in the larger society, lack sufficient prominence and contrastability to be useful for purposes of this study, however.

The Melting Pot Imagery and the Disillusionment with the Emigration Experience

By titling a novel *On the Way to the Melting Pot*, Waldemar Ager makes the melting pot symbolism a central element of his discussion.

A number of his articles revolve around the same concept. Ager disputes the host country's entitlement to the cultural assimilation of its new citizens and asserts that they owe their new homeland political allegiance but not their soul. In the context of the war, he adds that the state has the right to demand cooperation, but has no claim to control anyone's conscience.[40]

Ager argues that the melted-down American is less valuable to society than the immigrant newcomer. In the novel, he reverts the allegory to its practical origin:

> But he did not buy other people's machines to melt them down. He only melted down iron and scrap.... He used the melted scrap iron for the simplest part of his machine. He did not even use it for this purpose because he considered it the best, but because it was cheapest this way.[41]

With this concrete example Ager wants to warn his fellow immigrants against the melting pot. He surmises that, in spite of demanding assimilation, the American public does not respect immigrants who surrender their heritage and even prefers unassimilated newcomers. Through assimilation, the immigrants discard their own identity without being able to assume a new one.

The adverse side effects of emigration and acculturation lead to the inevitable question regarding the overall outcome of setting out to a new land. Did the gains outweigh the losses? Simon Johnson's immigrant patriarch Jens Braastad assails the rigid social hierarchy in the old country, where low social status stifles people's energy and prevents them from discovering their full potential. Braastad's prosperity on the prairie was based in part on the desire to prove that he, too, could succeed. His triumph would be complete if he had the opportunity to impress the highly born of his home village with his possessions. Other characters, such as his wife and his son, pay an emotional price for their lack of identity—a price that is even more obvious in Waldemar Ager's novel. Mrs. Skare, who can hardly communicate with her children, ultimately loses her sanity, and the old Morstuen couple, whose family has been dispersed all over North America, is troubled by hallucinations and loneliness. Thore Overhus is driven to suicide by his private alienation and his financial decline.

It is O. E. Rølvaag, however, who elaborates most on the cost of emigration. Dr. Green, reflecting on the broken spirits among his patients, declares in *Their Fathers' God* that winning the prairie came at too high a price. In his early work, *Amerika-breve* (America Letters), Rølvaag even develops a theoretical approach to the subject. This novel illustrates the extent to which Rølvaag's literary works reflect his cultural and political views, since Rølvaag integrates a speech he had given on 4 July 1911 in the little Norwegian-American settlement of Winger nearly verbatim into the fictitious story. He does not overlook the benefits reaped by his fellow immigrants. Through hard work, they had become wealthy. They had learned to work economically. They were enjoying the freedom and the countless opportunities offered by America.

Among the losses, Rølvaag lists intangibles more than anything else. Although he infers that many an emigrant might also have succeeded at home if he had labored as tirelessly as on the prairie, the loss of their country appears to be the real price. The beauties of Norwegian nature and the security of a community that is distinctly one's own are invaluable commodities that had to be sacrificed. Rølvaag speaks in the tradition of culture-based identity when he says:

> When we lost our fatherland we did not only become—as indicated before—strangers among strangers, but: *we parted from our own nation and became strangers to our own people.* Our pulse can no longer share our own people's heartbeat. We have become strangers. Strangers to the people we left, strangers to the people we came to. The fatherland to which we had a one-thousand-year-old right of inheritance we gave away, and we of the first generation cannot receive another one in its place.[42]

This is the price paid by the emigrant in Rølvaag's eyes. Therefore, Beret cannot return to Norway after Per Hansa's death, whereas Rønnevik sees return as a viable option and has his protagonist Lars Holte vicariously leave the New World again. Rølvaag argues that the emigrant is destined to remain forever rootless, a Flying Dutchman without a home in spite of his or her material possessions. It cannot come as a surprise that he regarded this price as too high.

7
Reception in the Norwegian-American Community

THE PRESERVATIONIST AUTHORS PURSUED POLITICAL GOALS IN addition to artistic ones. By investigating the reception their works received in the immigrant community, one can approximate the political and societal impact they had. An examination of the overall readership reached by individual novels and of the verifiable reaction traceable through reviews in Norwegian-American papers will serve this purpose. While the newspaper critics cannot lay claim to fully representing the community at large, their opinions, in combination with the sales figures, supply valuable insights.

In the American census of 1940, 658,220 residents reported Norwegian as their mother tongue.[1] At the time the four novels were published, this number was slightly higher, but the difference is not significant for the purposes of this study. By the same token, the number of Norwegian speakers reached by the various novels can only be approximated. Gudrun Hovde Gvåle states that Norwegian-American novels were usually printed in numbers of about 2000 to 3000 copies.[2] Rølvaag's earlier novels appeared in these numbers at the Lutheran-affiliated Augsburg Publishing House. The same publisher, in all probability, printed a similar edition of Simon Johnson's *Frihetens hjem*.

Ager and Rønnevik found themselves in different circumstances. Ager was in charge of the small Norwegian publishing house Fremad. While he printed only 750 copies of *Paa veien til smeltepotten*, he also serialized it in his newspaper *Reform*.[3] As *Reform* had a circulation of 5300 copies at the time, the novel's readership was multiplied by the serialization. Rønnevik, on the other hand, lacked not only his own printing facility but also an outside publisher. He brought out *100 procent* himself; years later he stated that he had broken even on his novel, even though he still had 300 copies in his basement.[4] These numbers indicate that a few hundred copies were sold.

The sales figures of Rølvaag's later novels were considerably higher, but the particular circumstances of their publication complicate the retrieval of readership data. The Norwegian edition of *Peder Seier* and *Den signede dag* was distributed by Aschehoug, a leading publishing house in Norway. Both books originally appeared in Norwegian in numbers of 7000 and 6000 copies, respectively, most of which were sold in Norway.[5] In Rølvaag's private correspondence, one finds information about the sale of the Norwegian edition in North America. Aschehoug sent 200 copies of *Peder Seier* to Augsburg Publishing House and more than 100 to Rølvaag's hometown of Northfield.[6] Various Scandinavian booksellers in the United States ordered a total of approximately 200 copies of *Den signede dag* immediately after its appearance and certainly purchased more later.[7] *Den signede dag* topped the best-seller list in *Nordisk Tidende* around Christmas of 1931.

Since many Norwegian-Americans in all likelihood bought the English version of the trilogy, establishment of Rølvaag's readership among them is difficult. The complete English edition sold for $7.50 in 1932, whereas readers had to pay $11 for the Norwegian one.[8] One should note that Rølvaag originally did not know if the Norwegian edition of his work would be available on the American market. Both *Peder Victorious* and *Their Fathers' God*, which were the titles of the English translations, reached the American best-seller list; 42,453 copies of *Peder Victorious* were sold during the first three months of its appearance.[9] While it is impossible to tell exactly how many of these readers were Norwegian-Americans, one can safely project that thousands but not tens of thousands of them purchased the books in Norwegian or English.

Supplemented with the observation that one purchased book on the average corresponds to more than one reader, these aforementioned numbers indicate the percentage of Norwegian-Americans reached by these books. It becomes clear that even successful novels were only read by a small portion of the target audience. Their circulation could not compete with opinion makers such as American newspapers, or even with popular Norwegian language magazines such as *Kvinnen og Hjemmet,* which sold 50,000 copies per issue in 1916.[10] As a consequence, their political impact was limited from the start. Literature can exercise influence on public opinion, particularly when cooperating with other societal forces. Newer forms of mass communication, most of all television, expose their audience to distinctive value systems to an even greater extent. Preservationist literature, on the other

Much of the Norwegian-American cultural debate took place on those pages:
A collection of Norwegian-American newspapers and journals.
Courtesy Norwegian-American Historical Association.

hand, which lacked significant outside support and had to compete with the overwhelming assimilatory tendencies of American society, fought a losing battle from the beginning.

Reviews represent the other major source of information on the reception achieved by Norwegian-American literature. One must bear in mind, however, that most reviews were composed by amateurs with an interest in literature, and anyone expecting a wide array of scholarly analysis will be disappointed. Italian-American writers complained about the dearth of competent reviews of their works as late as the 1960s and pointed to the drawbacks for advertisements and sales this entailed.[11] The situation was no better within the Norwegian immigrant community. Not only did its literary critics frequently lack the necessary theoretical knowledge, their personal acquaintance with the authors complicated an objective judgment. Simon Johnson, for example, never forgave Rølvaag for submitting a slightly ironic but good-natured review of *Frihetens hjem*. Rølvaag explains in their ensuing correspondence that he had taken the difficult situation faced by Norwegian-American writers into account and had moderated his objections to various aspects of the novel out of respect for Johnson's dedication to his people. Nevertheless, the relationship between these men, both immigrant writers and preservationists, never returned to its former cordialness because Johnson felt betrayed by his colleague.[12]

No critical institution existed in the Norwegian-American literary realm, but the lack of scholarship apparent in the literary criticism that originated within the immigrant community does not have a negative impact on the present study. On the contrary, a less scholarly response to a novel will probably mirror its reception in the general public more authentically than would an academic critique.

Not all available reviews of the novels examined in this study will be referred to because some of them do not supply information relevant to the subject. The volume of published reaction to the various novels varies considerably. Since all the writers possess a similar cultural agenda, however, this disparity does not distort the findings. It is the overall reaction to preservationist literature that must be examined, and the fundamental philosophical agreement among the four authors elicits comparable reactions to their cultural ideology.

Waldemar Ager had attained the unofficial honor of being the leading Norwegian-American writer with his novel *Kristus for Pilatus* (Christ before Pilate), published in 1910. When intense agitation against "foreign" influences marred the United States during the years of World War I, Ager felt challenged to produce a literary response. *Paa veien til smeltepotten* came out in 1917, first serialized in *Reform* and then as a book.

Carl G. O. Hansen, in his paper *Minneapolis Tidende*, calls the character descriptions in *Paa veien til smeltepotten* unsurpassed in Norwegian-American literature. With a few sentences, Ager manages to make his characters come alive for the reader. While praising the novel's stylistic presentation, Hansen is more critical of its contents. He admits that there indeed exist Norwegian-Americans of the type presented by Ager, but he protests the one-sidedness of his portrayal and blames Ager for ignoring the countless immigrant homes in which the children grow up as Americans without holding their parents or their culture in disdain.[13] Ager responds to this criticism in a letter to Hansen, in which he concedes that his depiction lacks universal validity and explains that he needed to create a congruous atmosphere in order to present a convincing message.[14]

Whereas Hansen expresses mixed feelings about the book, Ager's friend J. J. Skørdalsvold has only favorable comments in *Folkebladet*. Without paying much attention to theoretical or formal aspects, he lauds Ager for holding a mirror up to his fellow immigrants. He, too, feels that the author's portrayal lacks universal validity, but his response differs from Hansen's. He thinks the book could shake up those who discard their heritage, whereas the rest of the immigrant community should not see it as collective criticism directed at them.

Washington Posten also comments favorably on the novel. The reviewer recommends it as both entertainment and psychological study, as a satire lamenting the Norwegian cotter spirit.[15] *Nordmands-Forbundet* views the novel from a domestic, Norwegian perspective, but the magazine was also read in the United States. Its reviewer, F. G. Gade, is the only analyst to draw political conclusions from the novel. He wants to strengthen Norwegian national consciousness so that emigrants leaving Norway take a secure identity with them. If this intention could have been realized, a preservationist novel would have achieved a clearly measurable political impact.

The most interesting discussion of Ager's novel takes place in one of the foremost Norwegian-American papers, *Decorah-Posten*. The editor publishes two opposing views on the book and places himself as arbiter between them. Under the signature Ej., the first critic reproaches Ager for trying to prevent the process of Americanization by misrepresenting its consequences. He accuses him of wrongly labeling Anglo-Americans and their culture as British, whereas they actually represent the essence of an independent American culture. He defends the "melting pot" and redefines it as expressing not a physical but a spiritual process. This American spirit would not undermine the position of Norwegian culture in the new country.

Ager's fellow author O. A. Buslett could not have disagreed more. He himself had published an allegory against hasty assimilation under the title *Veien til Golden Gate* (The Road to Golden Gate) and now praises *Paa veien til smeltepotten* as not only interesting, but also as realistic to the point of reminding him of real-life experiences. According to Buslett, the immigrants would contribute to the Americanization of the whole country by preserving their best natural traits and integrating them into the new society. What is generally described as Americanization is really Anglicization, the author argues. He thanks Ager for holding up a mirror to his fellow countrymen, but he doubts they will be ready to buy a book that forces them to question their own behavior.

The editor comments on the two reviews as much as on the book itself. He argues that the other reviewers misunderstood the meaning of the novel and attempts to redefine its message. He sees two kinds of Americanization: a healthy one that benefits both the individual and society, and an unhealthy one in which the individual aimlessly discards his identity. The author surmises that Ager attacks Americanization only when it is unhealthy, because the process itself cannot be stopped. Buslett is blamed for trying to stand in the way of history, whereas Ager ostensibly pointed to the pitfalls of unhealthy Americanization. The editor concludes his article by recommending the book if it is understood in the right manner.

This interpretation of the novel demonstrates the difficulties faced by preservationist authors. Even when Norwegian-American newspapers try to refrain from open criticism, they can still undermine the message. Ager clearly agrees with Buslett in his rejection of cultural assimilation, but the paper turns his appeal for cultural preservation into an argument for wise assimilation. The review also reveals that Ager and his colleagues had to wage a battle on two fronts. They not only had to defend their cultural program against the majority society, but also had to face the opposition of assimilation-minded members of their own ethnic group.

Whereas *Paa veien til smeltepotten*, appearing in 1917 at the height of antiforeign sentiment, created a spirited debate about the validity of its judgment, *Frihetens hjem* aroused little political controversy. To a large extent, this can be attributed to the change in public opinion between 1917 and 1925, but the differences in basic sentiment that speak from the two novels must have mattered as well. Whereas Ager creates an unattractive portrayal of a Norwegian immigrant community, Johnson contrasts villains and shining knights, both taken from the same community. As a consequence, few readers felt personally attacked in Johnson's book.

In *Decorah-Posten*, the author and pastor H. A. Foss comments positively on *Frihetens hjem* without presenting much analysis of its contents. He briefly sums up the mood of dissatisfaction prevalent in the settlement described in the novel and stresses that Olaf Nelson and his wife distinguish themselves through their unassailable character and their faithfulness to both their ancestral homeland and their new country. Foss concludes by calling the novel a true mirror of prairie life and recommending it for both its historical and its entertainment value.[16]

J. J. Skørdalsvold's article in *Lutheraneren* likewise summarizes more than it analyzes. The critic indicates at one point that it requires patience to read through the extensive presentation of Olaf Nelson's exemplary views, but he hopes that the cultural preservationists, in particular, will value the book. Skørdalsvold refrains from commenting on the message of the novel, but between the lines, one notices reservations about the book.[17]

Whereas the first two reviews remain superficial and essentially recommend the book because it is written by a fellow Norwegian-American, John Heitmann examines it in more depth. Publishing under his pen name Bjarne Blehr in the *Duluth Skandinav*, Heitmann twice describes the novel as "peculiar."[18] He praises Johnson's mastery of the topic and the author's intellectual and emotional involvement in the story, commending Johnson for having spent much time and thought on the novel. When the review lists Olaf Nelson's impressive accomplishments, one cannot but notice the manifold exaggerations in the book, and Heitmann classifies it as a touching sermon. He wants to applaud at one moment and to protest in the next, but even when he disagrees with the author, he cannot but respect his firm conviction. Johnson manages to formulate many true statements in an elegant and convincing manner, and in spite of its lack of humor, the novel is entertaining reading. Heitmann concludes his review by hailing the deep emotional attachment to both Norway and the United States that speaks from the work.[19]

O. E. Rølvaag regularly reviewed the works of his fellow authors. In his critique of *Frihetens hjem*, he is torn between praise for the author's convictions and intentions and doubts about their artistic realization. He notices the romantic nature of a novel that revolves around an invincible knight in shining armor who not only defeats the scoundrels but also educates his wife and the reader about true virtue. Rølvaag would be inclined to understand the story as a parody if he did not know that Johnson never jokes about these matters. The reviewer does not fail to see the propagandistic potential of *Frihetens hjem* and values its contribution to the ongoing cultural debate, but he also recognizes that this very purpose limited its literary potential. The story does not speak directly to the reader—the author himself intervenes and preaches. In spite of pointing to a number of improbabilities in the plot, Rølvaag concludes that *Frihetens hjem* is an interesting and good book that Norwegian-Americans who are conscious of their heritage should read and recommend.

Simon Johnson did not appreciate Rølvaag's criticism, and his indignant complaints illustrate the disadvantages of having Norwegian-American books reviewed by fellow authors.[20] They all knew each other and hesitated to express negative opinions because they did not want to offend or discourage their colleagues.

Hans Rønnevik was disadvantaged in comparison to the other authors in this study. Having to publish one's novel oneself not only led to considerable expense but also deprived the author of the public relations network of major publishing houses. As a consequence, the chances of reaching a mass audience were diminutive. Rønnevik's situation was not unique, however, because many immigrant writers were forced to publish their works themselves.

O. E. Rølvaag reviews the novel in *Skandinaven* and calls it arguably the best debut novel ever to appear among Norwegian-Americans. Rølvaag praises the fact that the book manages to remain entertaining in spite of its serious content, which summons up unpleasant memories in many readers. He understands the author's bitterness about the naiveté displayed by the American public during the war but adds that the novel's impact could have been enhanced by utilizing irony instead of indignation.

This favorable review was confirmed by The Norwegian Society of America, which awarded Rønnevik its literary prize for the novel. In spite of this encouraging reception, Rønnevik was unable to publish further novels. Although he had manuscripts at home, he was restricted to shorter contributions to newspapers and magazines. His long life extended into an era when time had run out for Norwegian-American literature.

O. E. Rølvaag's last books received more attention than those of any other preservationist writer. He had become famous for *Giants in the Earth,* and the general audience wanted to hear more about the trials of the Holm family. Rølvaag's friend John Heitmann examined *Peder Seier* for the *Duluth Skandinav.* He calls it a true masterpiece without equal in world literature and ranks it higher than its famous predecessors in psychological depth, the clarity of its images, artistic form, and positive human sentiment. Rather than a scholarly response, Heitmann supplies an impressionistic one that defines *Peder Seier* as a book that makes one glad to be Norwegian.

Decorah-Posten also praises the novel, describing it as an angry book in which the political message nevertheless comes second to the artistic will. Rølvaag manages to cast light upon the sacrifices brought by the immigrants on their way to full membership in the American nation, an element that *Minneapolis Tidende* refers to as well. Through the English edition, the general American public will be able to understand what the often misused concept of Americanization really entails. The paper lauds the realism attained by the author and his success in avoiding any tendentiousness.

Norgesposten encourages all Norwegian-Americans to read this truthful portrayal of life in the pioneer days. The book is presented as both a psychological study and a contribution to contemporary political debate. Kristine Haugen, the mother of Rølvaag's later famous student, Einar Haugen, also recognizes the novel's historical accuracy. If it does not reach the literary heights of *Giants in the Earth,* she ascribes this fact to the more intricate social structure that has developed in the settlement and its demands for a broader, less intense portrayal. Her letter to *Nordisk Tidende* is more positive than the newspaper's official review, in which Rølvaag is criticized for painting too bleak a picture of Norwegian America. Beret is viewed in a negative light, accused of fanaticism in her resistance to Americanization, and called incapable of adjusting to the new country. The lack of understanding displayed for the main preservationist character and for the author's concern about the precarious state of the immigrant culture manifests the paper's assimilation-oriented sentiments.

Skandinaven also questions the general validity of Rølvaag's description—at least the way it had been interpreted by critics in Norway. Rølvaag has written a powerful epic, the reviewer stresses, but it must not be read as a history of Norwegian America. While the novel deserves the enthusiastic reception it received, one should not forget that it is fiction. *Scandia,* on the other hand, praises the work for its realistic depiction of an episode in the history of Norwegians in America. At the same time, the publication considers it one of the best psychological analyses ever written in Norwegian.

Waldemar Ager's critique in *Reform* is remarkably differentiated. The writer Ager underlines that Rølvaag writes fiction, not history. He calls it inappropriate to equate Peder Seier's religious views with Rølvaag's. This does not prevent him from calling Beret a spokesperson for the author's views on ethnicity. These seemingly contradictory elements add up to an important interpretation of Rølvaag's—and Ager's—preservationist novels. While not writing documentaries, the authors use their fictional characters for historical and ideological purposes. Ager would be able to understand the intertwining purposes better than any other critic, since he knew both Rølvaag and the literary process.

Ager compares the finale of *Giants in the Earth*, expressed by Per Hansa's death in the blizzard, to Beret's spiritual resignation before her son's marriage to an Irish Catholic at the conclusion of *Peder Seier* and indicates that the end of the story has not yet been reached. In an extensive analysis in *Normanden*, J. A. Holvik, on the other hand, regards Peder's marriage as a rather arbitrary conclusion. He agrees with Ager when he classifies Rølvaag's characters as individuals not as types. Holvik contests the prevalent view among American critics, who perceive Beret and Peder as prototypes of first- and second-generation Norwegian-Americans. He bases his rejection of this interpretation on Rølvaag himself, who denied that his characters represented types and negated the existence of general formulas in life. Rølvaag described his method of creating characters as the compression of numerous real-life impressions into new fictional personalities but conceded that these fictional characters serve as illustrations for historical interpretations. Holvik echoes these words when he dismisses the notion that Beret represents a typical representative of a first-generation pioneer but accepts her as a realistic defender of the immigrant heritage in fictional form. This differentiation remains useful today as a guideline for distilling historical source material from immigrant literature.

Lyder Undstad in *Reform* likewise praises Rølvaag's success at creating authentic personalities in his writings, calling him unique among Norwegian-American authors in this respect. Undstad views it as a sign of Rølvaag's great talent that he does not become a mere spokesperson for the Norwegian cause but leaves room for a variety of opinions within a realistic study of the immigrant community. The reviewer compares Rølvaag with Olaf Duun and generously predicts that both will eventually receive the Nobel Prize for Literature.

Unlike most other newspapers, *Lutheraneren* draws practical conclusions from Rølvaag's novel. The latter will undoubtedly have appreciated it when his readers went beyond recognizing his novel for its artistic value and contemplated the lesson contained in it. *Lutheraneren* acclaims Rølvaag's intimate knowledge of Norwegian-American history and his unmatched talent for transposing this knowledge into a truthful portrait of his ethnic group. This gift not only makes Rølvaag the leading Norwegian writer in North America but encourages a serious evaluation of the dangers he warns about, states the reviewer, who urges parents, priests, and teachers to study Peder's development and to learn from the mistakes made in his education. This was certainly the kind of reception Rølvaag himself desired for his novels.

The response to Rølvaag's last book, *Den signede dag,* was similar to the one received by its predecessor. Rølvaag's sudden death shortly after its appearance had to influence the public reception, however. Many reviewers commented on his authorship as a whole as much as on his final work, and a few critics chose to reinterpret parts of the novel rather than to criticize it.

When *Reform* first announces the appearance of *Den signede dag,* it praises the novel as Rølvaag's best since *I de dage.* *Skandinaven* goes even further, asserting that Rølvaag has reached the peak of his artistic mastery in it. The paper indicates that the book has become a best-seller and defends the author against criticism of the novel's historical authenticity by arguing that it is the obligation of the historian, not of the poet, to submit a comprehensive portrayal of Norwegian pioneer life.

John Heitmann in the *Duluth Skandinav* regards Rølvaag's last book as his psychological masterpiece. He has created real characters with good and bad sides, not heroes or saints, declares Heitmann, but he nevertheless has created a new picture of Norway in the eyes of the world. The Norwegian-Americans should be grateful for having been immortalized by Rølvaag, who has won them respect among their American fellow citizens.

Decorah-Posten quotes from reactions to the novel in Norway, where it was seen as fundamental for the understanding between Norwegians and their emigrated brethren and was praised both for its literary qualities and for the historical information it contained. No one who wants to study Norwegian-American history will be able to forgo Rølvaag's novels, *Decorah-Posten* cites the Norwegian writer Kristian Elster, and in its own review, the paper elaborates on the same statement. By entering the heart and mind of his characters, the author manages to impart to his readers an understanding beyond the one attainable from normal history books. In particular, he accomplishes the depiction of the difficulties and frustrations that accompany the assimilation process, personifying in Beret the tragedy of the emigrant people.

Minneapolis Tidende underlines the tragic aspects in Rølvaag's immigrant epic. The popular view of the melting pot likes to portray the expected final product, argues the paper, without considering the enormous costs along the way. Even if all the immigrants could eventually melt together into one indivisible nation, the spiritual price paid in the process might still be too high, and Rølvaag masterfully directs attention to this fact.

A few weeks later, the same paper takes another look at Rølvaag's final novel. This time it becomes clear that the critic does not share Rølvaag's cultural views. Instead of objecting to the author's message, he substantively reinterprets it. He states categorically that Rølvaag not only did not object to exogamous marriages but also used his novel to explain their inevitability. The reviewer argues that the union between Susie and Peder would have been happier if both sides had been able to discard their heritage more thoroughly and reduces Rølvaag's message to a statement about the time frame necessary to accomplish this. The marriage fails because of the spouses' incomplete assimilation according to this interpretation, which leaves room for a demand for accelerated assimilation and thereby clearly contradicts Rølvaag's intentions. The examination of Rølvaag's ideology establishes his unequivocal opposition to complete Americanization to the point of warning against a process that he might have accepted as inevitable.

Nordisk Tidende likewise transforms the author's message. Under the headline "The children of the pioneers run against the reef of religious prejudice," the paper views the marital conflict between Peder and Susie as predominantly religious in nature. When the critic uses the melting pot analogy that certain metals cannot be amalgamated, he equates chemical with sectarian incompatibility. He perceives Rølvaag's description as valid for the period alluded to—the 1890s—but expounds that religious conflicts have since lost much of their bitterness. The critic disregards the ethnic dimension in Rølvaag's novel, a dimension that was both current and visible. As in the previously mentioned review, it remains unclear whether the critic deliberately adjusted the book's message to his own worldview or if he sincerely understood it differently than most other critics.

After a few weeks, *Reform* published a second commentary on *Den signede dag*. Waldemar Ager interprets Rølvaag's message as "birds of a feather flock together," which expresses a fundamental ethnonationalist sentiment they both shared. The religious component is only one of the many expressions in the multifaceted complex of ethnicity. Ager also suggests that Rølvaag was not finished with Peder yet. Only the author's early death prevented him from concluding the development of this character, after his long illness had not been able to keep him from completing *Den signede dag*. Ager is convinced that Peder would have rediscovered his heritage—mainly through the community of thought and sentiment he experiences with Nikoline, the visitor from Peder's family's northern Norwegian home district.

A common thread discernible in the reviews is the extent to which they integrate these literary works into the contemporary cultural debate. Preservationists gladly turn to them as a source of ideas for their own arguments. Assimilationists, while hesitant about directly attacking co-ethnic literary figures, reinterpret the message or direct it away from issues of contention. The journalists feel obligated to support the authors—and both groups are not clearly separated—through positive reviews, but the most interesting aspect of the published responses is the personal involvement that speaks from them. These immigrant novels touched their readers, who felt attacked or affirmed by works of fiction. The audience judged these novels according to the way their descriptions related to the readers' impressions of reality—even though they knew they were reading fictional accounts. This demonstrates the political role and impact of this literature. It reformulated the contemporary debate in literary terms, and people reacted to it as part of this debate.

8
Ethnicity, Activism, and Literature—A Conclusion Put into Context

OPPONENTS OF ETHNIC PRESERVATIONISM IN THE UNITED STATES accused this intellectual tradition of harboring foreign allegiances and lacking American patriotism. They questioned the right of immigrants to remain in their chosen country if they seemed unwilling to assimilate into its existing structures. Based on Old World standards, these objections seem justified. Traditional societies had a foundation in a particular cultural legacy with special claims to the local territory; prospective immigrants could not be in doubt about the ethno-cultural parameters of the environment that awaited them.

Were the same standards applicable in the New World as well? Was the development toward the current cultural configuration of the United States predetermined and historically unalterable? While it remains difficult to answer the objective aspects of these questions because of the intrinsic speculativeness of alternative historical scenarios, enough evidence exists to underscore the subjective peculiarities of emigrating to the New World. For many earlier immigrants, America represented something new—they perceived the New World as a promise of land and freedom without envisioning an automatic surrender of traditions that remained dear to them. Later waves of immigrants, who arrived in a widely settled, urbanized country, did not necessarily share the same expectations, but as long as Europeans conceived of America as a continent to be won, its final cultural form remained undecided in the eyes of many of its settlers.

No ethnic group harbored such alternative conceptions of America more extensively than the Germans. They were by far the most numerous non-English speaking immigrant community throughout the nineteenth century, with roots going back to the colonial period, from which time language islands have survived in Pennsylvania to this day. During the 1800s, a constant flow of new immigrants settled the vast agricultural areas of the Midwest, covering this part of the United States with a dense network of German communities. Many of these pioneers intended to preserve their culture in the new environment. At various times they entertained plans to create a German state within the Union and contemplated Texas, Missouri, and Wisconsin as possible sites of this state. Regardless of their feasibility, these endeavors reveal the desire of at least part of the German community to allow for a culturally German expression of American identity. The proponents of such concepts did not want to preserve allegiances to foreign potentates, but considered a German expression of Americanism as legitimate as an English one—and able to coexist with it.

Ultimately, plans for the creation of a German state came to naught. The Norwegians, for their part, never dominated sizable areas of North America to the extent the Germans did. Nevertheless, Anglicization was not an automatic ingredient of every Norwegian immigrant's American dream. The Norwegians shared with the Germans an extensive participation in the actual cultivation of vast stretches of newly-won territory along the frontier. This experience of breaking the soil imparted a heightened conviction of an original claim to it. This land had not previously been settled by Anglo-Americans, so why should they have superior rights to it? This line of reasoning reassured ethnic preservationists of the justness of their demands for cultural autonomy. In those days, of course, the relevant group for comparison was seen in the Anglo-Americans and not in the American Indian population that represented the actual natives of these regions.[1]

Cultural identity did not have to be tied to a territorial base. In fact, ethnic identity—in its early manifestation as tribal affiliation—historically dominated an individual's state of belonging. In medieval Europe, legal status was determined by tribal background regardless of domicile; a Bavarian living in Frisia was subject to Bavarian, not to Frisian law. Only the increasing power of local princes gradually allowed them to enforce their expanding regulations on all the people within their domain. When the concept of the nation state seemed to demand the identity of territory and populace, subgroup autonomy was further reduced.

This historical excursion illustrates the historical basis of the preservationist expectation of a lasting reference group of Norwegian-Americans or German-Americans. Even in contemporary India, a person's identity as a Sikh, for example, will constitute a more significant frame of reference than his or her state or province of residence. Race forms an equally important constituent of identity formation in the United States. Werner Sollors calls the U.S.A. an unusually monolingual polyethnic country, indicating by the use of the modifier *unusually* that an alternative outcome would have seemed just as feasible.[2] North America has been a continent in constant flux; what seems natural today did not seem natural one hundred years ago, and what was taken for granted only a few decades ago is changing before our eyes.

When Margaret Mead postulated that all Americans view themselves as descendants of George Washington, who is an ancestor with whom one strives to belong, she drew attention to the perennial tension between the principles of consent and descent in the formulation of an American identity.[3] The intellectual dominance of the consent principle—defining America as the home of the free, to which all freedom-loving people of the earth can belong—has survived all of the inconsistencies and contradictions that have accompanied it. Descent does of course permeate American history, from African slavery to Asian exclusion to racial quotas, to cite only a few examples. At the same time, American national mythology has created an imaginary descent as an outgrowth of consent ideology. As an American, you descend from Washington even if your British ancestors fought against American independence, and the son of German immigrants participates in the glory of American victory in the World Wars even though his actual forefathers fought on the opposing side.

It is only logical that some immigrant thinkers—and not only they—have taken the consent principle to its ultimate conclusion. If you become an American by way of your consciousness, native-born Americans also may require Americanization. In *Frihetens hjem*, Simon Johnson uses this argument to protest the illiberal assimilation campaign of the 1910s, but in the real world it never achieved much significance—an indication of the practical limitations of the consent principle. Immigrants might argue that their spirit makes them real Americans—the average American tends to judge them by more pragmatic criteria, such as their accent.

This clash between different identity markers also appears within the Norwegian immigrant community. In response to the activist novel *Pa veien til smeltepotten*, a reviewer emphasized in 1917 that his fellow immigrants were accidentally born in Norway, whereas they had chosen America of their own free will, frequently having been Americans in spirit even before they set foot on its shores.[4] In addition to a spiritual definition of Americanism, this line of reasoning contains an unequivocal rejection of the descent principle by contrasting incidental birthplace with chosen domicile. In the preservationist conceptual framework, on the other hand, there is nothing incidental about someone's ancestral homeland. What preservationists would call the natural belonging—one is Norwegian because one was integrated into this culture through parents who had been acculturated the same way—in their eyes outweighs the acquired American one, which arguably can be achieved by anyone through a personal declaration of intent. The difference in terminology between natural versus (artificially) acquired, on the one side, and incidental versus self-chosen, on the other, illustrates the nearly insurmountable barriers between these opposing schools of thought.

The clash of philosophies transcends ethnic borderlines and leaves questions about the true antagonisms in American society. Upon viewing the often acerbic arguments *within* American ethnic and racial groups over the respective desirability of autonomous development and integration, one cannot avoid the impression that much of America's ethnic strife is actually a struggle between conflicting ideologies. Israel Zangwill faced at least as much opposition for his popularization of the melting pot metaphor within the Jewish community, where the philosopher Horace Kallen offered the imagery of an orchestra as his alternative to Zangwill's boiling cauldron, as in society at large.[5]

* * *

Myths permeate the discourse on group identity. The American myth of spiritual descent from sanctified founding fathers—itself rivaled by the equally American myth of purported biological descent from beatified arrivals on the Mayflower—finds equivalents in ethnic myths within immigrant communities. Irish activists traced the roots of representative government and other "American" traditions back to Ireland. They were convinced that America was discovered by the Celtic explorer St. Brendan, and they ascribed the defeat of the British in the Revolutionary War almost exclusively to Irish soldiers.[6]

The Scandinavians had their own mythology, which established their original claim to America. In its mixture of fact and fiction, the Viking discovery of North America is aided by the fanciful Kensington runestone, which a Scandinavian farmer claimed to have found on his Minnesota farm, and the established Norse identity of the early discoverer Leif Eriksson is combined with questionable assertions of

Columbus' Norwegian roots. These palpable aspects of the Scandinavian myth are accompanied by a more esoteric ideological superstructure, in which Scandinavia functions as the origin of democracy and liberty and the democratic tradition of Iceland is combined with the assertion that England's liberal institutions originated in its areas of dense Scandinavian settlement.[7]

The Scandinavian claim to liberty and self-government found resonance among American intellectuals, some of whom integrated Viking elements into their Anglo-Saxon view of history. As such it was accompanied—and rivaled—by the Teutonic myth, which located the origin of American political institutions in the forests of Germany, from which the migrating Anglo-Saxons had ultimately transplanted them to the New World.[8] This Germanic mythology is particularly useful for demonstrating the dangers inherent in generalized assumptions of inherited ideology, because the vagueness of the historical evidence allows for arbitrary interpretations in line with the spirit of the day. The forests of Germany, indeed, came to appear in noticeably less benevolent interpretations in subsequent decades. The Norwegian writer Sigrid Undset presented a fanciful explanation for differences between German and Norwegian culture by describing the former as determined by its origin in vast forests and the latter as shaped along the shores of the open sea. The Germans supposedly united into hordes to overcome their fear of the dark woods, whereas the Norwegians developed a spirit of independence and freedom through their individual mastery of the ocean. Undset, no friend of Germany and the Germans, designated the same forests that had been seen as the homeland of liberty and self-rule as the birthplace of a brutal horde mentality.[9] Along similar lines, the Nobel Prize-winning author Elias Canetti interpreted the forest with its powerful presence of large, erect trunks as a symbol of the Prussian army, equating the German love for their woods with a spirit of militarism.[10]

These curious examples of negative stereotyping would not deserve much attention if they did not represent the downside of much of ethnic mythology. If the very same forests serve as the unwitting origin of both liberty and oppression, other vague inheritances can change from blessing to curse. Will Italian-Americans, most of whom arrived in North America after the European conquest of the continent had been completed, be held responsible for their much celebrated fellow-Italian Christopher Columbus when his slowly emerging negative characterization as the originator of the destruction of Native-American culture turns him into an ethnic liability? Already, the spiritual descent of white America from its slave-holding founding fathers ties the American children of twentieth-century Ukrainian immigrants to the evils of American slavery, although their contemporary forefathers might have spent their lives as the serfs of Russian aristocrats. Mythic participation in historical American processes may lead to concepts of hereditary responsibility for Americans whose ancestors had not even had the opportunity to enjoy special privileges.

The attempt to establish preferential claims to America could also be based on assertions of special ancestral or spiritual ties to the country's Anglo-American majority. Norwegian-Americans stress this communality when O. E. Rølvaag expects President Coolidge, as an Anglo-American, to favor northern European immigration, or when the Scottish-American Dr. Green feels at home in the Puritan austerity of Beret Holm's farm in Rølvaag's widely read novel *Their Fathers' God*.[11] The central role ascribed to Anglo-Americans in these theories allowed them to play various groups against each other whenever it seemed in their own interest.

The experiences of the Germans, as the largest immigrant community, again supply the most descriptive examples. Along with the Scandinavians, the Germans also viewed themselves as ethnic relatives of the Anglo-Saxons, with special aptitudes for becoming Americans. They shared the opposition to the dramatic increase in immigration from eastern and southern Europe that began in the 1880s and defined themselves as part of a northern European, old-stock America. As indicated in the discussion of the Teutonic myth, their sentiments were echoed by parts of the Anglo-American establishment, and the acceptance of German Protestants in the American mainstream clearly lay above that of Catholic or Orthodox Slavs—until America entered World War I.[12]

In the course of that war, things were reversed: Germany was the enemy and German culture became transformed into an authoritarian antipode to American democracy. The subsequent time period witnessed coalitions of Anglo-Americans and Slavs in the name of international brotherhood versus the alleged agents of German imperialism. The Slavs had turned into defenders of democracy and cooperated with the Anglo-Saxons in the curtailing of German-American ethnic expression. Chicago, in particular, experienced a wave of renamings of German topographic and street names. Deep-seated resentments among the Slavic second-class outsiders turned against the German first-class outsiders. The outcome only benefited the Anglo-American majority, because the suppression of the most powerful proponents of cultural pluralism aided the complete dominance of English monolingualism and deprived the Slavic communities, too, of any hope for cultural survival.[13]

These events contribute to an understanding of the underlying reasons for the successful Anglicization of the large American immigrant population. The various ethnic communities rarely defined themselves as a union of non-English speakers collectively interested in defending their individual identities against the American mainstream. More often than not, they jealously guarded their particular interests by attempting to establish a preferential claim to the country based on historical or political affinities to the majority population. Each ethnic group tended to be more concerned about perceived privileges of other immigrant groups than about the gradual absorption of all immigrants into the majority society.

Due to their relative lack of power both within and outside the United States, the Scandinavians were never seen as a significant threat, sparing them the most traumatic experiences of the Germans. The historical and religious affinities between the two groups blurred their distinctions in the eyes of many Americans, however, and before long all non-English speakers had become the target of Americanization fever during World War I.[14] Simon Johnson expressed his frustration about this development, because in his ardent ethnic particularism, he had at first approved of the curtailing of German-American activities without fully appreciating that it initiated measures against all forms of cultural pluralism. Lack of interethnic unity was not the decisive factor for the ultimate failure of cultural preservationism, but it contributed to its rapid collapse. The lack of comprehensive solidarity did not exclude the possibility of limited ethnic cooperation, and in contrast to Simon Johnson's position, Norwegian-Americans frequently empathized with their German neighbors. Norwegian-American political and cultural leaders, as well as a number of authors, such as Hans Rønnevik and Hans Foss, expressed this uneasiness among many Norwegians about the rather simplistic portrayal of both Germany and German-Americans that was so prevalent during World War I.

* * *

Religion and ethnicity were deeply intertwined in the history of most American immigrant groups. In some cases, the connection was obvious—as in the case of the Jews or of nationalities that had their exclusive ethnic Church, such as the Armenians. In other instances, the relationship was less overt, but religion formed a significant part of the cultural tradition of virtually all immigrant communities. The religious liberties guaranteed in the United States enabled the various denominations to develop institutional structures along ethnic lines without the interference from the government experienced by similar nonreligious institutions. Consequently, religious bodies often played a role in the preservation of immigrant culture that considerably exceeded their cultural importance in the home country.

The religious history of Norwegian-Americans supplies important information about the northern European ethno-religious experience in the New World. Norwegians were almost exclusively Lutherans, but they formed only one segment of the Lutheran population in the United States. As a consequence, the Lutheran Church served as a protector of Norwegian ethnicity as long as it remained divided along cultural lines, whereas it developed an integrative role as soon as these barriers had come down. In reverence of its original role, Waldemar Ager defended the Church against the visiting Norwegian writer Bjørnstjerne Bjørnson, who had critized the societal influence of the Norwegian-Lutheran clergy in the United States in public lectures to the Norwegian-American community, and pointed out that the Church had been instrumental in preserving the Norwegian language in the new country.[15]

Heinz Kloss summarized the role of the Lutheran Church-Missouri Synod for German preservationism in a manner that can be directly applied to the Norwegian situation. He maintained that the Missouri Synod had done more for the German language than any other institution but that the language as such was irrelevant to the Church and only served as a means to further its religious mission.[16] Initially, Norwegian-Lutheran religious bodies also viewed the language barrier as necessary for the shielding of their members from the rationalism prevalent in the American Protestant denominations and from the materialism in American society at large. In the settlement period, Norwegian-Lutheran religious leaders were concerned that the faithful would surrender their religious traditions together with their cultural ones and would join American churches once they had become assimilated.[17]

With the increase in American-born members, concerns began to change, and Church officials feared that the younger generation would desert them unless a switch to English occurred. Whereas the Norwegian language seemed an asset in the settlement period, it was now viewed as a liability, and a gradual but rapidly accelerating replacement of Norwegian by English took place in the subsequently united Norwegian-Lutheran Church. Preservationists reacted with confusion and anger at the perceived betrayal of their cause by its most important proponent. Two letters published in the Norwegian language newspaper *Duluth Skandinav* on 5 May 1922 illustrate the opposing sentiments and could be supplemented by countless similar statements. Whereas a supporter of the changes views them as the sole chance for the survival of the Church because the younger generation would otherwise join English denominations, an opponent calls on Norwegian-Americans to protest against the new policy. He accuses the Church of closing Norwegian religious schools by pretending not to find teachers for them and perceives an organized attempt at undermining the future of Norwegian within the Lutheran Church.

The bitterness among preservationists was based on a misunderstanding of the Church's original motives for its support of Norwegian institutions. As Kloss pointed out for the Missourians, the Church only supported the immigrant language as long as it served its spiritual mission. Its initial cultural role among the Norwegians led to an almost complete lack of secular structures in the service of language preservation—Norwegian America was predominantly organized in its churches. Out of the 1.5 million Norwegian-Americans of his time, Carl G. O. Hansen estimated that approximately 60,000 were members of Norwegian associations. Even though Odd Lovoll regards this number as too low, no estimate puts it even near the total of 500,000 Norwegian Lutherans.[18] The Church, however, made no secret about its priorities, as can be seen in a 1922 editorial in its official organ, *Lutheraneren*:

> The language question is primarily a local question to be decided in each case based on the local conditions. The only consideration should be the demands of the religious mission in the respective area. The Church has nothing to do with the preservation of the Norwegian language and culture. The Church has nothing to do with language change and Americanization. The Church is not a servant of the languages; it will use the languages, and, depending on the local conditions, it will serve the people in one or several languages.[19]

The reliance on religious structures tied the fate of Norwegian America almost exclusively to an increasingly nonethnic institution. In the more diverse German-American community, which was not only divided into numerous religious denominations but also contained a vocal element of freethinkers, no such exclusive dependency developed. Kloss' estimate for 1930 of two million Germans organized in ethnic churches and of a corresponding number of members of secular associations assumes equally strong blocs of *Kirchendeutsche* (church-Germans) and *Vereinsdeutsche* (association-Germans).[20] This diversity impeded attempts at having the German element in the United States speak with one voice in political questions, but it widened the organizational foundations of the language maintenance efforts.

A distinction between church-Norwegians and association-Norwegians would have limited methodological value because of the numerical imbalance between the two groups, but it is worth remembering that almost two-thirds of Norwegian America remained outside either secular or religious ethnic institutions. This reminder illustrates that even the broad-based language debate within the Lutheran Church lacks general validity for the complete Norwegian-American community.

An interesting aspect of Norwegian-American cultural life lies in the high degree of symbolic ethnicity that has survived within this group. While German-Americans had once developed extensive secular structures in defense of their language, those ultimately unsuccessful endeavors were not followed by an equally comprehensive associational life for acculturated Americans of German descent. Norwegian-Americans generally preserved more emotional attachment to their ancestral homeland, and organizations that express this symbolic ethnicity, such as the Sons of Norway, remain popular even among later generations. While some of the explanation for the relative weakness of comparable German organizations can be found in the political adversities faced by German-Americans in the course of this century, Norwegians also surpass Danes and Swedes in this respect.[21]

Scholars disagree about the true ideological designation of cultural preservationism. In Norway, opposing schools of thought placed Rølvaag in either an American or a Norwegian tradition. This dichotomous exclusiveness underestimates the potential for transnational synthesis. Mirroring the changed manifestation of ethnicity in the American environment, cultural preservationism reflects the imagery of ethnic nationhood placed in an immigrant context. In its new surroundings, this worldview did not express itself in its traditional manner, namely, the national awakening and mobilization of a territory's indigenous majority population. The reference group of cultural preservationists was their ethnic community, and in the defense of its identity, they retained European notions of culture-based identity as much as they formulated an alternative view of American cultural realities. While the numerous parallels between their goals and those of activists from other immigrant communities underline the American context of their activities, these Norwegian-American intellectuals cannot be understood without reference to their personal frame of allegiance. Rølvaag, Ager, and others may be able to inspire preservationists of different backgrounds, but they were not theory-minded cultural pluralists for the mere sake of principle. They were motivated first and foremost by dedication to their particular heritage, not by general notions about the organization of American society. Viewing these ethnic activists only as Americans neglects the driving force that inspired and motivated them. Insisting on classifying them either as Americans or as Norwegians would overlook the basic principles of their thinking, which rejected the notion of the state as the only frame of reference.

The interest of Norwegian-American activists in cultural pluralism almost certainly would have diminished after the demise of the Norwegian-American community; therefore, one cannot simply declare the recent resurgence of ethnic awareness in other American immigrant communities a belated victory for these Norwegian intellectuals. Their ideas might have been rediscovered, but Norwegian America in the sense they understood and desired it is a thing of the past.

* * *

How could literature contribute to the momentous historical developments that shaped America? Rølvaag predicted that Norwegian-American literature was destined to become valuable source material for later historians. Only literature would be able to provide insight into the immigrants' feelings. The elemental experience of assimilation into a new culture contains more subjective, emotional, inward-oriented aspects than objectively measurable ones. Writers legitimately saw a role for themselves in the exploration of these topics. Rølvaag maintained that an intelligent person would be able to read a people's spirit through its literature in the same way a botanist could judge the soil quality of an area from the plant life it supported. Without literature, one would not be able to discover what lay deep within Norwegian America.

Literary authors undoubtedly contribute to our understanding of the immigrant psyche, but they also confront the researcher with the problem of separating fact from fiction. Rølvaag integrated most of an actual Norwegian Constitution Day speech into his novel *Amerikabreve,* thereby blending an authentic event into a work of fiction. On other occasions, however, a novel's plot can become forced and unrealistic in order to accommodate the author's intentions. The plumber in Ager's *Paa veien til smeltepotten* is so obviously drawn as an example to be emulated by the reader that his authenticity suffers. In spite of his limited education and means, he is the only immigrant to attract and marry a woman from an Anglo-American middle-class background. Whereas the purely Norwegian families discard their heritage, this mixed marriage is bicultural—the plumber's American wife appreciates both the Norwegian language and the literature written in it. While not impossible, the combination of desirable traits is overwhelming.

Simon Johnson goes even further. The manner in which his protagonist Olaf Nelson turns his court investigation into a tribunal over assimilationism is only matched by the unique tolerance and understanding demonstrated by the patriotic American judge. In reality, dissenters found little sympathy in American courthouses during World War I, and Johnson's depiction of a contemporary investigation does not reflect the dangers involved in opposing America's loyalty crusade. Examples like these underscore that the usefulness of immigrant literature for historical purposes has its limits.

Lack of historical accuracy need not be based on intentional misrepresentation. The author might indeed be convinced that he portrays a situation truthfully—without genuinely accomplishing this feat. How difficult the task could be may be learned from the diverse reaction to Rølvaag's treatment of the Catholic Church in his immigrant trilogy. Critics from today's secular Norway, such as Ingeborg Kongslien, miss a portrayal of Susie's heritage that is as artful and thorough as that extended to Peder's. Rølvaag's editor, Eugene Saxton, viewed Peder as intellectually and emotionally set against Catholicism and indicated a desire to have him express his underlying thoughts in order to avoid the impression of sheer bigotry. Einar Haugen, on the other hand, whose background as a Midwestern Norwegian-American was similar to the author's, maintained that Rølvaag's treatment of the different denominations was evenhanded. Haugen's judgment makes it easier to understand the author's intentions. Rølvaag seriously tried to be fair to Catholicism, but his orthodox Lutheran upbringing in those days still proved an obstacle. It came more naturally for Rølvaag to assail Catholic rituals than Lutheran ones; they were less sanctified and more foreign to him. Consequently, the novel will be less valuable for its description of Catholic thinking in the early twentieth century than for its insights into Lutheran attitudes toward the Catholic Church at that time.

The ever-present danger of misinterpretation warrants a cautious use of historical conclusions. Rølvaag's protagonist, Peder Seier, has been described by critics as everything from an intolerant brute to an exemplary Norwegian-American and a born leader. The assessment of Peder's role in the author's concept forms a significant element in the analysis of the message, and the reliability of the interpretative judgment attains a particular significance when fiction is used as historical evidence.

Immigrant authors laid special claim to providing information on the emotional costs of assimilation, which they viewed as an aspect of American history that could not be reconstructed from other sources. Their novels abound with characters that were broken by their transplantation and could not achieve happiness in their new country. At the least, the members of the immigrant generation exhausted themselves laying the groundwork for later generations' success. Rølvaag was not the only one who regarded the price paid by his fellow immigrants for their material advancement as too high.

Were these sentiments representative of the average immigrant? Did the immigrant authors really understand the mind-set of the people they portrayed? Did these writers truly express the opinions of the farmers they were describing, or do the tensions and upheavals in the lives of their characters primarily represent a projection of the authors' own experiences? Most common people seem not to have shared the sense of tragedy in the emigration and assimilation process to the same extent as did these ethnic intellectuals. Their goals and desires revolved around more materialistic concepts, and their economic accomplishments contributed to a basic satisfaction with their situation. One has to distinguish between the issues of authenticity and representativeness. There can be no doubt that a segment of the immigrant population felt that the cultural loss outweighed the material gains or at least put their worth into question: the authors themselves prove the existence of these considerations. Even if one were to agree with the preservationists' assessment of the relative value of material and spiritual well-being, however, it might still remain questionable whether the average Norwegian immigrant depicted in the novels would have shared the authors' frustrations to the extent indicated. The fact that Waldemar Ager subjected many of his characters to a series of economic disasters suggests that he, too, suspected that his readers would not fully understand their predicament unless it was accompanied by material losses.

Werner Sollors describes this aspect of historical unreliability in his analysis of James Weldon Johnson's *Autobiography of an Ex-Colored Man* and Abraham Cahan's *The Rise of David Levinsky*. Both are fictional autobiographies of economically successful members of a minority group (one African-American, one Jewish), who confess to having betrayed their inner selves in order to succeed in an alien world. Sollors points out that "when visionaries write fictional autobiographies of invented practical men, it is perhaps not too surprising that these practical men suffer dearly from not having become visionaries."[22] These businessmen feel and speak like their idealist authors, who became ethnic activists. The frustration experienced by assimilated group members represents a projection of the author's own feelings about his characters. Transferred to the Norwegian situation: if Ager were Omley, he would feel like a failure, but a real-life Omley probably would not.

Only a minority experienced the surrender of ethnic traditions as an indignity. The German-American poet Victor G. Wicke expressed his frustration about this reality in the same time period:

> Viele sah ich englisch fälschen
> ihre deutschen Namen.—Selten
> können mehr als kauderwelschen,
> die als deutsch nicht wollen gelten.[23]

The difficulties surrounding ethnic literature as historical source material are connected to its involvement in the cultural debate. From the outset it should be clarified that political purpose does not in itself diminish the literary quality of a text. The interwar cultural left in Europe developed a whole genre of *Tendenzliteratur*. Scott de Francesco defined *Tendenz* as "distinguishable from propaganda because it is not force-fed polemic worked out from direct party-motivated guidelines. Tendentious literature teaches the reader to *see* for him- or herself."[24] Mainstream conservatives have been less inclined to accept the value of political literature because a powerful wing of conservative thought views existing conditions as the result of a predestined development and considers ideology an unnecessary or dangerous interference with the natural order of things. However, culturally conservative groups that were dissatisfied with the status quo developed their own literature, and in America these groups frequently had a Christian orientation.

Ager and Johnson started their careers in the Prohibition movement, which at that time represented the most vociferous expression of politicized, mainly Protestant, Christianity. Johnson, in particular, never completely managed to liberate himself from the moralist black and white imagery acquired during those years. Rølvaag, with his academic background, preferred a more complex interpretation of reality. This stylistic disagreement resulted in an argument with Simon Johnson, who felt betrayed when Rølvaag faulted *Frihetens hjem* for its extensive preaching and author interference. Rølvaag suggested that the author should have let the story speak for itself, yet Johnson saw this criticism as an outgrowth of subjective literary preferences and defended his style:

> My modest opinion is also that one should not dismiss too easily that which you call chatting and preaching. If one wants to solve the problem of treating thoughts and ideas artistically, one finds out soon that there are limited possibilities. Garborg can serve as an example here. Take his play *Læraren* (The Teacher), take *Heimkomen Son* (The Returned Son) and *Den burtkomne faderen* (The Lost Father), and you can take other ones too. That's sermonizing, my friend![25]

This debate demonstrates the artistic differences between two authors who worked for the same cause. Both Rølvaag and Johnson attempted to support the continuous existence of a separate Norwegian-American identity through their literary works, but they disagreed about the best manner of using this medium. The overlapping of literary and political considerations complicated an open debate about the quality of Norwegian-American literature, because fellow writers within this small community knew each other personally and frequently felt the need to support another author's cultural agenda with a positive review. Rølvaag tellingly informs Johnson that his criticism of *Frihetens hjem* would have been much harsher if he had not been impressed by the author's dedication to their common heritage.

The analysis of a text's message is further complicated by the influence of the author's purely personal ambitions and goals upon his literary production. Even activist authors do not work only for their ideals, but also to fulfill their personal dreams and aspirations. Rølvaag espoused a cause, but he also desired to be recognized as an author. Nowhere can this dichotomy express itself more confusingly than in the prehistory of his immigrant trilogy. True recognition of a Norwegian writer had to come from Norway, so Rølvaag continually searched for a Norwegian publisher. Indeed, *I de dage* and its successors were published by Aschehoug in Oslo, not by a Norwegian-American company. Can it be said, then, that these novels were written for Norwegian America? Their content expressed the author's views on ethnicity and immigrant culture, and there can be little doubt that Rølvaag wanted his fellow immigrants to be inspired by these works; but when they appeared in Oslo, he could not be sure they would become easily accessible in the United States. The large success of the trilogy and its translation into English finally disseminated its message among Norwegian-Americans, yet this outcome was not guaranteed. There remains the paradox that a Norwegian-American author writes a novel that contains an appeal to his immigrant community, only to have it published in the ancestral homeland because of the prestige involved. It will be easier to understand him if one considers the fact that fame in Norway would also reflect on a writer's standing in Norwegian America. Nevertheless, it can be justifiably concluded that preservationist authors did not sacrifice themselves on the altar of their cause but were human beings with personal interests and aspirations.

* * *

More than six decades after the appearance of the Norwegian-American writings examined in this study, the *New York Times* published an article describing the experiences of recent immigrants to America. The resemblance to events depicted in early twentieth-century Norwegian-American literature is striking. Parents from Russia and South America lament being corrected by their children, who speak better English than they do. They are proud of the ease with which their children adapt to the new country, but they also regret the impending loss of their own culture. Little has changed in the life of an immigrant over the course of this century.[26]

At the same time, a look into today's immigrant classrooms shows that there are hardly any Norwegians and few Europeans in them. A definition of American identity has become even more complicated over the last decades. Whereas Rølvaag still posed the rhetorical question to his assimilationist opponents whether they would have become Turks if their parents had emigrated to Turkey, Norway itself is today trying to define the status of the children of Turkish immigrants. During Rølvaag's time, the concept of "American" was still widely seen as a reflection of old-stock colonial American, but the demographic changes affecting the United States today are fundamentally redefining the country's identity. An assimilated European will no longer possess a claim to being uniquely American, yet he or she will not have the security of an established ethnicity to fall back upon, either. Norwegian immigrants expected to join a European-defined American mainstream by surrendering their heritage, but this type of mainstream might be disappearing. Today, some white Americans complain about the blandness of an American middle-class culture that could be viewed as the logical result of the leveling of countless immigrant heritages; they watch with fascination how non-Europeans integrate their distinct attributes into a new and more multifaceted America.

The loss of genuine ancestral tradition has been compensated to a certain extent by the development of a symbolic form of ethnicity. This development has become the true expression of Hansen's third-generation law, which holds that the third immigrant generation wants to remember what the second one wanted to forget.[27] While the assimilated generations have not actually revived their heritage, they have symbolically re-embraced it. In the long run, even this symbolism might be doomed, however. Ethnic recollections are most noticeable in the Northeast and the Midwest, where self-sufficient European communities still existed in living people's memory. Increasing generational distance and intermarriage will further undermine the foundation of anything but arbitrary self-identification.

In the 1980 U.S. census, 52 percent of the respondents listed a single, dominant ancestry. At the same time, 16 percent of whites indicated American or no ethnic background.[28] This group's particularly strong representation among Americans who have been in the country for more than four generations reinforces the assumption that its numbers will grow. Optimistic assessments of the continuance of immigrant culture among descendants of Europeans in the United States frequently overlook the minimal time period that has passed since the disintegration of vibrant European ethnic life in North America. As long as people with concrete memories of flourishing ethnic subcultures still dwell among us, predictions of a permanent establishment even of limited ethnic traditions seem premature.

The examination of symbolic ethnic identification also allows an evaluation of the impact achieved by ethnic activism and its literature. National pride has made a difference in the preservation of immigrant identity, as illustrated by the Icelanders on the Manitoba prairies. Aided by relative rural isolation, but hampered by low overall numbers, these Icelanders used their high educational standards and a strong sense of identity to preserve their native heritage longer than many other Northern Europeans.

Immigrant literature can also contribute to the continuance of symbolic loyalties. The literary documentation of group presence—particularly during the settlement period—enhances the desirability of group identification. Rølvaag's successful novels evoke ethnic pride both through the author—a Norwegian immigrant who became accepted into the American literary pantheon—and through their subject matter, which immortalized the Norwegian participation in the colonization of the prairies.

In spite of having enhanced the communal self-confidence of Norwegian-Americans, preservationists have also been the subject of controversy. Not only political opponents accused them of delaying the integration of the immigrant population into the mainstream in order to preserve them as their personal political and economic power base. The fact that Rølvaag originally published his immigrant trilogy in Norway has been referred to, and Waldemar Ager seems to confirm the suspicions of his opponents when he admits:

> Our newspapers, congregations and associations are all dependent on the preservation and cultivation of love to Norway and everything Norwegian. No one wants to cut off the branch on which he in a way has built his nest.[29]

Nevertheless, it would be wrong to interpret the intentions of Norwegian-American activists as predominantly self-serving. Preservationism attracted people with strong character who loved their heritage and suffered from its demise. Moreover, life as an activist was far from lucrative. If these immigrant intellectuals had only had their economic well-being in mind, their undisputed talents could have been used more profitably. Ager's statement indicates, however, how economic considerations influenced ethnic activists once they had entered a career within the communal structure of the immigrant group. Having invested the best years of their lives in the development of ethnic newspapers and associations, these immigrant leaders had tied their personal fortunes to the cultural survival of their immigrant community. This dependency on communal institutions made activists vulnerable to criticism that questioned their personal motives and interests.

While preservationist authors did not draw much material gain from their activities, they seem to have achieved a degree of personal satisfaction. Waldemar Ager confessed that he enjoyed speaking his mind, even if the ultimate impact was limited. Their literary production gave these authors the peace of mind derived from the fact that they had done everything within their power to influence the course of history. If Norwegian-America faded away, it would not be for lack of warnings.

Literary treatment of cultural dilemmas does not always aid their positive solution, however, least of all if the fictional text—contrary to reality—provides a happy ending. If the novel solves the problem for the reader, the latter can become complacent and forego personal involvement. It is possible that some authors made themselves and their audience feel better by creating an alternative outcome to a struggle they seemed to be losing in the real world. Simon Johnson's novels are most likely to prompt this interpretation. When Olaf Nelson addresses his opponents in court, one can almost visualize the author himself unloading his pent-up emotions and contemplations. Contrary to reality, both the American judge and the general public are not only swayed by Olaf's pleas for cultural pluralism but turn him into a folk hero. This reception stands in stark contrast to the loyalty campaign and the legal and extralegal harassment of imaginary spies and traitors that was so common during World War I. Olaf's triumph was a beautiful fantasy created for Norwegian-American preservationists.

What was ultimately accomplished by Norwegian-American activists and their literary writings? It has already been indicated that the creation of alternative historical scenarios, the liberating feeling of having spoken one's mind, and the public acknowledgment as a literary figure provided personal satisfaction for the writers. The literature failed to stop the tide of assimilation, but in their hearts, the authors foresaw this development. A close reading of their literary and nonliterary texts demonstrates that these immigrant intellectuals knew that they were fighting with their backs against the wall. In spite of arguing for the viability of a permanent Norwegian-American subculture, their works regularly betray an air of resignation. They, nevertheless, may have supported the continuing identification of many Norwegian-Americans with their ancestral heritage by supplying some of the positive symbols that are so instrumental for the particular kind of ethnic remembrance that currently predominates among Americans of European descent.

Literature also preserved the historical memory of life in

8: ETHNICITY, ACTIVISM, AND LITERATURE

Norwegian-America and documented the group presence in pioneer America. Few other sources can match the detailed description of the specific Norwegian contribution to the nineteenth-century settlement and cultivation of the North American prairies. Since mainstream American historiography rarely acknowledges the distinctly non-English flavor of the pioneer Midwest, a contemporary documentation from within the immigrant community becomes all the more valuable.

The documentary importance of this literature does not justify its uncritical use as historical source material, however. By expressing the ideas and sentiments of Norwegian-American preservationists, these works become a primary source of *Ideengeschichte*. They require, however, a careful contrastive analysis of their factual component. They provide an insight into Norwegian-America as seen through the eyes of its most ardent supporters, illustrating their sentiments in view of an ongoing assimilation process. They show how imaginative literature becomes a continuation of political discourse through other means. While they cannot be called primary sociohistoric source material and require analysis and interpretation based on additional evidence, they undeniably report *one* history of Norwegian America, *one* image of America, *one* American dream.

Notes

Chapter 1. Introduction to Norwegian-America and Its Literary Image

1. This and other widely known general historical facts will not be individually referenced. They can be be found in the historical works listed in the bibliography. A particularly helpful introduction to the topic is Odd Lovoll's *The Promise of America*.

2. James P. Nelson, "The Problem of Cultural Identity in the Works of Waldemar Ager, Simon Johnson, and Johannes B. Wist" (Ph.D. diss., University of Washington, 1990), 30.

3. Joshua Fishman, *Language Loyalty in the United States: The Maintenance and Perpetuation of Non-English Mother Tongues by American Ethnic and Religious Groups* (The Hague, 1966), 42.

4. Einar Haugen, *The Norwegian Language in America*, 2d ed. (Bloomington, Ind., 1969), 263–68.

5. Fishman, *Language Loyalty*, 58.

6. Hans Norman and Harald Runblom, *Transatlantic Connections: Nordic Migration to the New World after 1800* (Oslo, 1987), 246.

7. Haugen, *Norwegian Language*, 260.

8. Milton Gordon, *Assimilation in American Life: The Role of Race, Religion and National Origin* (New York, 1964), 71.

9. Recently, Elliot Barkan, in "Race, Religion, and Nationality in American Society," *Journal of American Immigration History* 14 (Winter 1995): 38–75, placed the Scandinavian-American population largely in stage five of his six-stage model of assimilation, ranging from contact via acculturation, adaptation, accomodation, and integration to full assimilation.

10. This and other theoretical works discussed in this section are listed fully in the bibliography.

11. Nathan Glazer and Daniel P. Moynihan, *Beyond the Melting Pot* (Cambridge, Mass., 1963).

12. This concept is reflected in the title of one of his publications: Werner Sollors, ed., *The Invention of Ethnicity* (New York, 1989).

13. Gans expresses his views most succinctly in his own contribution: Herbert Gans, ed., *On the Making of Americans* (Philadelphia, 1979).

14. Odd Lovoll, *The Promise of America: A History of the Norwegian-American People* (Minneapolis, 1984), 114.

15. Ibid., 122–26.

16. The terms *ethnic literature* and *immigrant literature* are not always clearly separated in this study because its scope is literature by immigrants, which forms a subsegment of ethnic literature. Immigrant literature is ethnic literature, but not all of ethnic literature is immigrant literature. Conclusions referring to ethnic literature in a study of immigrant literature, therefore, do not comprise a claim of general identity of these two concepts.

17. See, in particular, Hayden White, *Tropics of Discourse* (Baltimore, 1978).

18. Dorothy Burton Skårdal, *The Divided Heart: Scandinavian Immigrant Experience through Literary Sources* (Lincoln, Nebr., 1974), 19.

19. William Boelhower, *Through a Glass Darkly: Ethnic Semiosis in American Literature*, 2d ed. (New York, 1987), 133.

20. Werner Sollors, *Beyond Ethnicity: Consent and Descent in American Culture* (New York, 1986), 243.

21. Einar Haugen, *Ole Edvart Rølvaag* (Boston, 1983), 11.

22. Skårdal, *Divided Heart*, 40.

23. Hassels' novel was serialized in the Norwegian-American magazine *For Hjemmet* between June and October of 1874. For Anderson and Boyeson, see the bibliography.

24. Göran Stockenström, "Sociological Aspects of Swedish-American Literature," in *Perspectives on Swedish Immigration*, ed. Nils Hasselmo (Duluth, Minn., 1978), 268.

25. Norman and Runblom, *Transatlantic Connections*, 258.

26. The Norwegian name of the society was *Det Norske Selskab i Amerika*.

27. The goal aspired to was to investigate the topic both comprehensively and concisely, that is, not to leave out anything that is necessary nor to include information irrelevant to the examination of the question. It would have been easier to relate the entire plot of each of the novels examined, but this would not have supplied additional information about the writers' cultural ideology. On the other hand, it has been necessary to reproduce basic elements of the texts because they are not widely known and virtually inaccessible to an English-speaking audience. Biographical and other peripheral information, however, is easily available in other sources and has been limited here to the minimum necessary for an understanding of the subject. The analytical structure puts ethnic activism at the center of investigation, not specific novels or authors; therefore, the results should not primarily be seen in the context of literary biography or textuality.

28. The study is structured in the following manner: The first chapter supplies an introduction to the cultural and historical background of Norwegian-American literature and explains purpose and methodology. It is followed by the four chapters that analyze the individual works. By juxtaposing the treatment of relevant issues in both literary and nonliterary sources,

the sixth chapter develops the preservationist message that manifests itself in the authors' writings. Chapter 7 examines the response of the immigrant community as seen in the number of copies sold and in the published reaction. In the final chapter, the findings from these different analyses are drawn together into a general conclusion.

Chapter 2. Assailing the Melting Pot—Waldemar Ager

1. *Eau Claire Daily Telegram,* 1 August 1941.
2. Carl H. Chrislock, Ethnicity Challenged: *The Upper Midwest Norwegian-American Experience in World War I* (Northfield, Minn., 1981), 81.
3. Following the usage of the time period, the designation native or native American refers to people born in the United States of British background or assimilated into Anglo-American culture. Since the relationship between immigrants and nonimmigrants is concerned, this usage seems most sensible. This is particularly the case, since American Indians, i. e., Native Americans in today's usage, do not play a significant role in this study.

Chapter 3. Simon Johnson: A Chronicler of His Time

1. Simon Johnson, *Frihetens Hjem* (Minneapolis, 1925), 9. The translation of this and other non-English sources is my own unless the reference itself refers to a translated source.
2. Ibid., 348–49.

Chapter 4. Hans Rønnevik's Answer to the Loyalism Campaign

1. Hans Rønnevik to Einar Lund, Winneshiek County Historical Society Archives W 193:898–99, Luther College Library, Decorah, Iowa.
2. His idiom *at skjære alle* under *en kam* (on page 9, he cuts people "under" one comb, while correct Norwegian demands "over") is just one example.

Chapter 5. Wheat and Potatoes—Ethnic and Religious Differences in O. E. Rølvaag's Immigrant Trilogy

1. In Norwegian, the final two novels were titled *Peder Seier* (Peder Victory, 1928) and *Den signede dag* (The Blessed Day, 1931). *Giants in the*

Earth was divided into two separate volumes and *Peder Seier* and *Den signede dag* became volumes three and four in a tetralogy.

2. Ole E. Rølvaag, *Peder Seier*, new and rev. ed. (Oslo, 1977), 174. I am using my own translations of the original Norwegian text, not the freely translated and not always identical English version of the novel.

Chapter 6. Preservationist Ideas in Fiction and in Political Discourse

1. Einar Haugen, *Ole Edvart Rölvaag* (Boston, 1983), 6.
2. Gudrun Hovde Gvåle, *Ole Edvart Rølvaag: Nordmann og Amerikanar* (Oslo, Norway, 1962), 229.
3. Waldemar Ager, *Paa veien til smeltepotten* (Eau Claire, Wis., 1917), 33.
4. Ibid., 112.
5. Ibid., 195.
6. Odd S. Lovoll, ed., *Cultural Pluralism versus Assimilation: The Views of Waldemar Ager* (Northfield, Minn., 1977), 51.
7. Ibid., 72.
8. Rølvaag, *Peder Seier*, 177.
9. Ibid., 155–56.
10. Ole E. Rølvaag, *Omkring fædrearven* (Northfield, Minn., 1922), 72.
11. Ager, *Smeltepotten*, 18.
12. Ibid., 265.
13. Rølvaag, *Peder Seier*, 173–74.
14. Ole E. Rølvaag, "Norskens stilling," *Skandinaven*, 23 May 1911.
15. Ibid.
16. Ibid.
17. Waldemar Ager, "Vore frænder hinsides havet," *Kvartalskrift* 2:11 (April 1905): 24.
18. Waldemar Ager, "Den store udjævning IV," *Kvartalskrift* 9:16 (1920): 13.
19. Ager, *Smeltepotten*, 205.
20. "Sprogsaken," *Lutheraneren* (Minneapolis, 1922): 1104–5.
21. Lovoll, *Cultural Pluralism*, 56.
22. Ager, "Udjævning," 14.
23. Waldemar Ager, "Norskhetsbevegelsen i Amerika," *Nordmands-Forbundet* 18 (1925): 216.
24. Lovoll, *Cultural Pluralism*, 59.
25. Ager, *Smeltepotten*, 7.
26. Chrislock, *Ethnicity Challenged*, 54.
27. Lovoll, *Cultural Pluralism*, 79–80.
28. Ager, *Smeltepotten*, 6.
29. Ager, "Vore frænder," 21.

30. Lovoll, *Cultural Pluralism*, 102.
31. Gudrun Hovde Gvåle, *O. E. Rølvaag: Nordmann og Amerikanar* (Oslo, 1962), 239–40.
32. Johnson, *Frihetens hjem*, 276.
33. Hans Rønnevik, *100 Procent* (Carlisle, Minn., 1926), 101.
34. Ibid., 37.
35. The *odalsrett* tries to ensure that a family farm would be passed on from one generation to the next within the family and, therefore, grants special rights to family members. An *odalsgård* is a farm protected by this legal tradition.
36. Ager, "Vore frænder," 30.
37. Gvåle, *Rølvaag*, 228.
38. Rølvaag, *Fædrearven*, 173.
39. Simon Johnson, "Oplevd," Simon Johnson Papers, NAHA Archives, St. Olaf College Library, Northfield, Minn., 144.
40. Lovoll, *Cultural Pluralism*, 122.
41. Ager, *Smeltepotten*, 237.
42. Paal Mørck [Ole E. Rølvaag], *Amerika-breve* (Minneapolis, 1912), 170–71.

Chapter 7. Reception in the Norwegian-American Community

1. Haugen, *Norwegian Language*, 281.
2. Gvåle, *Rølvaag*, 289.
3. Waldemar Ager to Ole Buslett, 17 January 1918, Ole Buslett Papers, NAHA Archives, St. Olaf College Library, Northfield, Minn.
4. Hans Rønnevik to Einar Lund, Winneshiek County Historical Society Archives W 193: 898–99, Luther College Library, Decorah, Iowa.
5. *Northfield (Minn.) Manitou Messenger*, 11 December 1928.
6. Aschehoug Publishing House to Ole E. Rølvaag, 3 October 1928, Ole E. Rølvaag Papers, NAHA Archives, St. Olaf College Library, Northfield, Minn.
7. Aschehoug Publishing House to Ole E. Rølvaag, 21 October 1931, Rølvaag Papers.
8. *Nordisk Tidende* best-seller list, Rølvaag Papers.
9. Eugene Saxton to Ole E. Rølvaag, 10 April 1929, Rølvaag Papers.
10. *American Newspaper Annual & Directory 1916*, N. W. Ayer & Sons, (Philadelphia, 1916), 1284.
11. John M. Cammett, ed., *The Italian-American Novel* (New York, 1969), 27.
12. The correspondence between the two writers can be found in the Simon Johnson Papers and in the Ole E. Rølvaag Papers at the NAHA Archives at St. Olaf College.

13. The reviews of Ager's books can be found in the Waldemar Ager Papers, the reviews of Rønnevik's and Rølvaag's in the Ole E. Rølvaag Papers; all are located in the NAHA Archives at the St. Olaf College Library.
14. Einar Haugen, *Immigrant Idealist: A Literary Biography of Waldemar Ager, Norwegian American* (Northfield, Minn., 1989), 95.
15. Ibid.
16. *Decorah-Posten*, 16 March 1926.
17. *Lutheraneren* 9 (1925): 1421.
18. The identity of Blehr and Heitmann was first pointed out to me by Orm Øverland and later confirmed in a letter written by Rølvaag.
19. *Duluth Skandinav*, 11 December 1925.
20. Their exchange is discussed in greater detail in the final chapter.

Chapter 8. Ethnicity, Activism, and Literature—A Conclusion Put into Context

1. This aspect draws attention to the fact that European-American immigrant ethnicity tends to see the white American mainstream as its "other"; for the relationship to nonwhites, ethnicity is less of an issue. Native-Americans or African-Americans, for their part, would also see Norwegian-Americans as whites more than as Norwegians.
2. Sollors, *Beyond Ethnicity*, 39. In his reaction to the Americanization drive of World War I, Kallen suggested that the United States establish themselves as a federation of nationalities that would cooperate harmoniously. Kallen's essay "Democracy versus the Melting Pot: A Study of Amerian Nationality," which first appeared in *The Nation* in February 1915, never influenced the public debate to the extent Zangwill's play did.
3. Margaret Mead, *And Keep Your Powder Dry: An Anthropologist Looks at America*, new ed. (New York, 1965), 49.
4. *Decorah-Posten*, 27 November 1917.
5. Sollors, *Beyond Ethnicity*, 97.
6. Maxine Seller, *To Seek America—A History of Ethnic Life in the United States* (Englewood Cliffs, N.J., 1988), 102.
7. Valuable documentation of this Scandinavian mythology can be found in Dag Blanck, "Constructing an Ethnic Identity: The Case of the Swedish-Americans," in *The Ethnic Enigma*, ed. Peter Kivisto (Philadelphia, 1989), 134–52. An original source is Ole E. Rølvaag's, *Omkring fædrearven* (Northfield, Minn., 1922).
8. The thesis of the German origins of liberal institutions can be traced back as far as Montesquieu.
9. See Borghild Krane, *Sigrid Undset: Liv og meninger* (Oslo, 1970), 266.
10. Elias Canetti, *Masse und Macht*, new ed. (Munich, 1993), 202.
11. Ole E. Rølvaag, *Their Fathers' God*, trans. Trygve Ager, reprint (Westport, Conn., 1976), 241.

12. Kathleen Neils Conzen refers to nineteenth-century German-Americans as seeing themselves destined to codominate America with the Anglo-Americans; Kathleen Neils Conzen, "German-Americans and the Invention of Ethnicity," in *America and the Germans*, ed. Frank Trommler and Joseph McVeigh (Philadelphia, 1985), I:141.

13. Ample documentation of this changed image of German-Americans can be found in Frederick Luebke, *Bonds of Loyalty: German-Americans and World War I* (DeKalb, Ill., 1974).

14. The impact of World War I on the Norwegian-American community is explored in Carl Chrislock's *Ethnicity Challenged: The Upper Midwest Norwegian-American Experience in World War I* (Northfield, Minn., 1981).

15. Waldemar Ager, "Vore frænder hinsides havet," *Kvartalskrift* 9:16 (1920): 13.

16. Heinz Kloss, *Um die Einigung des Deutschamerikanertums* (Berlin, 1937), 80.

17. For a discussion of early Norwegian Synod attitudes, see Odd Lovoll, *The Promise of America* (Minneapolis, 1984), 67–69.

18. Odd Lovoll, *Cultural Pluralism versus Assimilation: The Views of Waldemar Ager* (Northfield, Minn., 1977), 17.

19. "Sprogsaken," *Lutheraneren* (Minneapolis, 1922): 1104.

20. Kloss, *Einigung*, 34.

21. Odd Lovoll argues that Norwegian-Americans have preserved more of their cultural uniqueness in general than have other Scandinavians. See Odd Lovoll, *The Promise of America* (Minneapolis, 1985), 212f.

22. Sollors, *Beyond Ethnicity*, 172.

23. Ernst Jockers, ed., *Deutsch-Amerikanischer Musenalmanach* (New York, 1925), 174. The prose translation of the verse is as follows: Many I saw falsify their German names to English. Rarely can those who do not want to be seen as Germans more than gibber [in English].

24. Scott de Francesco, *Scandinavian Cultural Radicalism* (New York, 1990), 55.

25. Simon Johnson to Ole E. Rølvaag, 10 March 1926, Rølvaag Papers.

26. Sara Rimer, "In the Race to Speak English, Pride Is Tinged with a Sense of Impending Loss," *New York Times*, 19 January 1992, 16.

27. Marcus Lee Hansen, "The Third Generation in America," *Commentary* XIV (November 1952): 492–500.

28. Peter Kivisto and Dag Blanck, eds., *American Immigrants and Their Generations* (Chicago, 1990), 73–74.

29. Ager, "Vore frænder," 21.

Bibliography

Ager, Waldemar. *Paa drikkeondets konto: Fortællinger og vers*. Eau Claire, Wis., 1894.
———. *I strømmen*. Eau Claire, Wis., 1899.
———. *Afholdssmuler fra boghylden*. Eau Claire, Wis., 1901.
———. *Fortellinger for Eyvind*. Eau Claire, Wis., 1905.
———. *Hverdagsfolk*. Eau Claire, Wis., 1908.
———. *Kristus for Pilatus*. Eau Claire, Wis., 1910.
———. *Fortællinger og skisser*. Eau Claire, Wis., 1913.
———. *Paa veien til smeltepotten*. Eau Claire, Wis., 1917.
———. *Udvalgte fortællinger*. Minneapolis, 1918.
———. *Ny samling fortællinger og skisser*. Eau Claire, Wis., 1921.
———. *Det veldige navn*. Eau Claire, Wis., 1923.
———. *Gamlelandets sønner*. Oslo, 1926.
———. *Hundeøyne*. Oslo, 1929.
———. *Under forvandlingens tegn*. Eau Claire, Wis., 1930.
———. *Skyldfolk og andre*. Eau Claire, Wis., 1938.
Alba, Richard. *Ethnic Identity: The Transformation of White America*. New Haven, Conn., 1990.
Andersen, Arlow. *The Immigrant Takes His Stand: The Norwegian-American Press and Public Affairs, 1847–1872*. Northfield, Minn., 1953.
Anderson, Benedict. *Imagined Communities: Reflections on the Origins and Spread of Nationalism*. London, 1983.
Anderson, Rasmus B. *America not Discovered by Columbus*. Chicago, 1874.
Askevold, Bernt. "Nogle tanker om norskheden i Amerika." *Symra* 4 (1908): 60–66.
Balan, Jars, ed. *Ethnicity and the Writer in Canada*. Edmonton, Alberta, 1982.
Barkan, Elliot. "Race, Religion, and Nationality in American Society." *Journal of American Immigration History* 14 (Winter 1995): 38–75.
Barth, Fredrik. *Ethnic Groups and Boundaries*. Boston, 1969.
Bernard, Richard M. *The Melting Pot and the Altar: Marital Assimilation in Early Twentieth-Century Wisconsin*. Minneapolis, 1980.

Bjork, Kenneth. *West of the Great Divide: Norwegian Migration to the Pacific Coast, 1847–1893*. Northfield, Minn., 1958.

Blegen, Theodore C. *Norwegian Migration to America, 1825–1860*. Northfield, Minn., 1931.

———. *Norwegian Emigrant Songs and Ballads*. Minneapolis, 1936.

———. *Norwegian Migration to America: The American Transition*. Northfield, Minn., 1940.

———. *Amerikabrev*. Oslo, 1958.

Bodnar, John. *The Transplanted: A History of Immigrants in Urban America*. Bloomington, Ind., 1985.

———. *Remaking America: Public Memory, Commemoration, and Patriotism in the Twentieth Century*. Princeton, N.J., 1992.

Boelhower, William. "The Immigrant Novel as Genre." *MELUS* 8 (Spring 1981): 3–13.

———. *Through a Glass Darkly: Ethnic Semiosis in American Literature*. New York, 1987.

Boyeson, Hjalmar Hjorth. *Gunnar: A Tale of Norse Life*. Boston, 1874.

Brye, David. "Wisconsin Scandinavians and Progressivism, 1900–1950." *Norwegian-American Studies* 27 (1977): 163–93.

Buslett, Ole A. *Veien til Golden Gate*. Northland, Wisc., 1915.

Cahan, Abraham. *The Rise of David Levinsky*. New York, 1917.

Cammett, John M., ed. *The Italian-American Novel*. New York, 1969.

Canetti, Elias. *Masse und Macht*. New ed. Munich, 1993.

Chrislock, Carl H. *The Progressive Era in Minnesota, 1899–1918*. St. Paul, Minn., 1971.

———. "Name Change and the Church." *Norwegian-American Studies* 27 (1977): 194–223.

———. *Ethnicity Challenged: The Upper Midwest Norwegian-American Experience in World War I*. Northfield, Minn., 1981.

Christianson, John R., ed. *Scandinavians in America: Literary Life*. Decorah, Iowa, 1985.

Connor, Walker. *Ethnonationalism*. Princeton, N.J., 1994.

Conzen, Kathleen Neils. *Immigrant Milwaukee, 1836–1860*. Cambridge, Mass., 1976.

Conzen, Kathleen Neils, et al. "The Invention of Ethnicity: A Perspective from the U.S.A." *Altreitalie* 3 (April 1990): 37–62.

Daniels, Roger. *Coming to America: A History of Immigration and Ethnicity in American Life*. New York, 1991.

Davis, Horace B. *Toward a Marxist Theory of Nationalism*. New York, 1978.

Davis, Lennard J. *Resisting Novels: Ideology and Fiction*. New York, 1987.

De Francesco, Scott. *Scandinavian Cultural Radicalism: Literary Commitment and the Collective Novel.* New York, 1990.

De Vos, George, and Lola Romanucci-Ross, eds. *Ethnic Identity: Cultural Continuities and Change.* Palo Alto, Calif., 1975.

Di Pietro, Robert, and Edward Ifkovic, eds. *Ethnic Perspectives in American Literature: Selected Essays on the European Contribution.* New York, 1971.

Draxten, Nina. *Kristofer Janson in America.* Boston, 1976.

———. *The Testing of M. Falk Gjertsen.* Northfield, Minn., 1988.

Eckstein, Neil T. "The Social Criticism of Ole Edvart Rölvaag." *Norwegian-American Studies* 24 (1970): 112–36.

Fishman, Joshua. *Language Loyalty in the United States: The Maintenance and Perpetuation of Non-English Mother Tongues by American Ethnic and Religious Groups.* The Hague, The Netherlands, 1966.

Fishman, Joshua, ed. *The Rise and Fall of the Ethnic Revival.* Berlin, 1985.

Flatin, Kjetil A. "Historisk roman-emigrantroman. Genrespørsmål i tre norske verk om utvandringa til Amerika." *Edda* (1977): 157–70.

Foss, Hans A. *Valborg.* Decorah, Iowa, 1927.

Frye, Northrop. *Anatomy of Criticism.* New York, 1966.

Fuchs, Lawrence. *The American Kaleidoscope: Race, Ethnicity, and the Civic Culture.* Hanover, N.H., 1990.

Gans, Herbert, ed. *On the Making of Americans.* Philadelphia, 1979.

Geertz, Clifford. *The Interpretation of Cultures: Selected Essays.* New York, 1973.

Gieske, Millard, and Steven Keillor. *Norwegian Yankee: Knute Nelson and the Failure of American Politics, 1860–1923.* Northfield, Minn., 1995.

Gjerde, Jon. *From Peasants to Farmers: The Migration from Balestrand, Norway, to the Upper Middle West.* New York, 1985.

Glasrud, Clarence. *Hjalmar Hjorth Boyesen.* Northfield, Minn., 1963.

Glazer, Nathan, and Daniel P. Moynihan. *Beyond the Melting Pot: The Negroes, Puerto Ricans, Jews, Italians, and Irish of New York City.* Cambridge, Mass., 1963.

Glazer, Nathan, and Daniel P. Moynihan, eds. *Ethnicity.* Cambridge, Mass., 1975.

Glicksburg, Charles I. *The Literature of Commitment.* Lewisburg, Pa., 1976.

Gordon, Milton. *Assimilation in American Life: The Role of Race, Religion and National Origin.* New York, 1964.

Greeley, Andrew. *Ethnicity in the United States: A Preliminary Reconnaissance.* New York, 1974.

Green, Rose Basile. *The Italian American Novel: A Document of the Interaction of Two Cultures.* Cranbury, N.J., 1974.

Greene, Victor. *American Immigrant Leaders, 1800–1910: Marginality and Identity.* Baltimore, 1987.

Gross, Theodore L., ed. *A Nation of Nations: Ethnic Literature in America.* New York, 1971.

Gulliksen, Øyvind T. "In Defense of a Norwegian-American Culture: Waldemar Ager's *Sons of the Old Country.*" *American Studies in Scandinavia* 19 (1987): 39–52.

Gulliksen, Øyvind T., Ingeborg R. Kongslien, and Dina Tolfsby, eds. *Essays on Norwegian-American Literature and History.* Vol. 2. Oslo, 1990.

Guttmann, Allen. *The Jewish Writer in America.* New York, 1971.

Gvåle, Gudrun Hovde. *Ole Edvart Rølvaag: Nordmann og Amerikanar.* Oslo, 1962.

Halvorsen, Hazel. "The Norwegian Heritage in America: Rölvaag's Concern for a Pluralistic Society." Master's thesis, South Dakota State University, 1974.

Hambro, Johan, ed. *De tok et Norge med seg. Nordmanns-forbundets saga gjennom 50 år.* Oslo, 1957.

Handlin, Oscar. *The Uprooted: The Epic Story of the Great Migration that Made the American People.* Boston, 1951.

———, ed. *Immigration as a Factor in American History.* Englewood Cliffs, N.J., 1959.

Hasselmo, Nils. *Amerikasvenska.* Stockholm, 1974.

———. *Swedish America: An Introduction.* Minneapolis, 1976.

———. ed. *Perspectives on Swedish Immigration.* Chicago, 1978.

Haugen, Einar. *The Norwegian Language in America: A Study in Bilingual Behavior.* 2 vols. Bloomington, Ind., 1969.

———. *Ole Edvart Rölvaag.* Boston, 1983.

———. *Immigrant Idealist: A Literary Biography of Waldemar Ager, Norwegian American.* Northfield, Minn., 1989.

Herberg, Will. *Protestant-Catholic-Jew: An Essay in American Religious Sociology.* Rev. ed. Garden City, N.Y., 1960.

Hicks, George, and Philip Leis, eds. *Ethnic Encounters: Identities and Contexts.* North Scituate, Mass., 1977.

Higham, John. *Strangers in the Land: Patterns of American Nativism, 1860–1925.* New York, 1974.

———, ed. *Ethnic Leadership in America.* Baltimore, 1978.

Hobsbawm, Eric, and Terrance Ranger, eds. *The Invention of Tradition.* Cambridge, 1983.

Hoerder, Dirk, ed. *Distant Magnets: Expectations and Realities in the Immigrant Experience, 1840–1930.* New York, 1993.

Hollinger, David. "How Wide the Circle of 'We'? American Intellectuals and the Problem of the Ethnos since World War II." *American Historical Review* 98 (April 1993): 317–37.

Holmquist, June, ed. *They Chose Minnesota: A Survey of the State's Ethnic Groups.* St. Paul, 1981.

Houe, Poul, ed. *Out of Scandinavia: Essays on Transatlantic Crossings of Cultural Boundaries.* Minneapolis, 1993.

Hovde, Oivind, and Martha E. Henzler, eds. *Norwegian-American Newspapers in Luther College Library.* Decorah, Iowa, 1975.

Hraba, Joseph. *American Ethnicity.* Itasca, Ill., 1979.

Hustvedt, Lloyd. *Rasmus Bjørn Anderson: Pioneer Scholar.* Northfield, Minn., 1966.

Hutchinson, E. P. *Immigrants and Their Children, 1850–1950.* New York, 1956.

Hvidt, Kristian. *Flight to America: The Social Background of 300,000 Danish Emigrants.* New York, 1975.

———, ed. *Emigration fra Norden indtil 1. verdenskrig.* Copenhagen, 1971.

Isaacs, Harold. *Idols of the Tribe.* New York, 1975.

Iser, Wolfgang. *The Act of Reading: A Theory of Aesthetic Response.* Baltimore, 1978.

Iverslie, Peter P. "Ogsa lidt om norskarbeidet." *Symra* 9 (1913): 251–54.

Jaeger, Luther. "Norskarbeidet og ungdommen." *Symra* 9 (1913): 171–73.

Jauss, Hans Robert. *Toward an Aesthetic of Reception.* Minneapolis, 1982.

Jenswold, John. "Becoming Americans, Becoming Suburban: Norwegians in the 1920s." *Norwegian-American Studies* 33 (1992): 3–26.

Johnson, James Weldon. *The Autobiography of an Ex-Colored Man.* In *Three Negro Classics,* introd. John Hope Franklin. New York, 1965.

Johnson, Simon. *Et geni.* Eau Claire, Wis., 1907.

———. *Lonea.* Eau Claire, Wis., 1909.

———. *I et nyt rige.* Minneapolis, 1914.

———. *Fire fortællinger.* Minneapolis, 1917.

———. *Fallitten paa Braastad.* Minneapolis, 1922.

———. *Frihetens hjem.* Minneapolis, 1925.

Jorgenson, Theodore, and Nora Solum. *Ole Edvart Rølvaag: A Biography.* New York, 1939.

Kälvemark, Ann-Sofie, ed. *Utvandring. Den svenska emigrationen til Amerika i historiskt perspektiv.* Stockholm, 1973.

Kazal, Russell. "Revisiting Assimilation: The Rise, Fall, and Reappraisal of a Concept in American Ethnic History." *American Historical Review* 100:2 (April 1995): 437–71.

Kero, Reino. "The Novel as a Source of History." *American Studies in Scandinavia* 16 (1984): 81–84.

Kerst, Catherine. *Ethnic Folklife*. Washington, D.C., 1987.

Kilde, Clarence. "Tragedy in the Life and Writings of Waldemar Ager, Norwegian Immigrant, Author and Editor, 1869–1941." Master's thesis, University of Minnesota, 1978.

———. "Dark Decade: The Declining Years of Waldemar Ager." *Norwegian-American Studies* 28 (1979): 157–91.

Kivisto, Peter, ed. *The Ethnic Enigma*. Philadelphia, 1989.

Kivisto, Peter, and Dag Blanck, eds. *American Immigrants and Their Generations*. Urbana, Ill., 1990.

Klein, Karl Kurt. *Literaturgeschichte des Deutschtums im Ausland*. Leipzig, Germany, 1939; reprint, Hildesheim, Germany, 1979.

Klein, Marcus. *Foreigners: The Making of American Literature 1900–1940*. Chicago, 1981.

Kloss, Heinz. *Um die Einigung des Deutschamerikanertums*. Berlin, Germany, 1937.

———. *The American Bilingual Tradition*. Rowley, Mass., 1969.

———. *Grundfragen der Ethnopolitik: Die Sprachgemeinschaften zwischen Recht und Gewalt*. Vienna, Austria, 1969.

Kongslien, Ingeborg. *Draumen om fridom og jord*. Oslo, Norway, 1989.

Krane, Borghild. *Sigrid Undset: Liv og meninger*. Oslo, Norway, 1970.

Kvamme, Kristen. "Norskarbeidet og kirken." *Symra* 9 (1913): 110–15.

Lecomte, Monique, and Claudine Thomas, eds. *Le facteur ethnique aux Etats-Unis et au Canada*. Lille, France, 1983.

Leiren, Terje. *Marcus Thrane: A Norwegian Radical in America*. Northfield, Minn., 1987.

Lindmark, Sture. *Swedish America, 1914–1932: Studies in Ethnicity with Emphasis on Illinois and Minnesota*. Uppsala, Sweden, 1971.

Lovoll, Odd S. *A Folk Epic: The Bygdelag in America*. Boston, 1975.

———. *The Promise of America*. Minneapolis, 1984.

———. *A Century of Urban Life: The Norwegians in Chicago before 1930*. Urbana, Ill., 1988.

———, ed. *Cultural Pluralism versus Assimilation: The Views of Waldemar Ager*. Northfield, Minn., 1977.

———, ed. *Makers of an American Immigrant Legacy*. Northfield, Minn., 1980.

———, ed. *Nordics in America*. Northfield, Minn., 1993.

Lovoll, Odd S., and Kenneth Bjork. *The Norwegian-American Historical Association, 1925–1975*. Northfield, Minn., 1975.

Luebke, Frederick. *Bonds of Loyalty: German-Americans and World War I*. DeKalb, Ill., 1974.

———, ed. *Ethnicity on the Great Plains*. Lincoln, Nebr., 1980.

Mann, Arthur. *The One and the Many: Reflections on the American Identity*. Chicago, 1979.

Mannsaker, Jørund. *Emigrasjon og diktning. Utvandringa til Nord-Amerika i norsk skjønnlitteratur*. Oslo, 1971.

Marzio, Peter, ed. *A Nation of Nations*. New York, 1976.

Marzolf, Marion. *The Danish-Language Press in America*. New York, 1979.

Mccabe, Cynthia. *The Golden Door: Artist-Immigrants of America, 1876–1976*. Washington, D.C., 1976.

Mead, Margaret. *And Keep Your Powder Dry: An Anthropologist Looks at America*. New York, 1965.

Meyer, Roy W. *The Middle Western Farm Novel in the Twentieth Century*. Lincoln, Nebr., 1965.

Morawska, Ewa. "In Defense of the Assimilation Model." *Journal of American Ethnic History* 13 (Winter 1994): 76–87.

Morlan, Robert. *Political Prairie Fire: The Nonpartisan League, 1915–1922*. Minneapolis, 1955.

Mortensen, Wayne F. "The Problem of Loss of Culture in Rölvaag's *Giants in the Earth, Peder Victorious,* and *Their Fathers' God.*" *Minnesota English Journal* 8 (Winter 1972): 42–51.

Moseley, Ann. *Ole Edvart Rølvaag*. Boise, Idaho, 1987.

Mossberg, Christer Lennart. *Scandinavian Immigrant Literature*. Boise, Idaho, 1981.

Munch, Peter A. "Segregation and Assimilation of Norwegian Settlements in Wisconsin." *Norwegian-American Studies and Records* 18 (1954): 102–40.

Naess, Harald S. *Knut Hamsun og Amerika*. Oslo, 1969.

———, ed. *Norwegian Influence on the Upper Midwest*. Duluth, Minn., 1976.

Nelson, E. Clifford, and Eugene L. Fevold. *The Lutheran Church among Norwegian-Americans: A History of the Evangelical Lutheran Church*. 2 vols. Minneapolis, 1960.

Nelson, Frank. "The School Controversy among Norwegian Immigrants." *Norwegian-American Studies* 26 (1974): 206–19.

Nelson, James. P. "The Problem of Cultural Identity in the Works of Waldemar Ager, Simon Johnson, and Johannes B. Wist." Ph.D. diss., University of Washington, 1990.

Newman, Katherine D. *The American Equation: Literature in a Multi-Ethnic Culture*. Boston, 1971.

Nielsen, George. *The Danish Americans*. Boston, 1981.

Norborg, C. Sverre. *An American Saga*. Minneapolis, 1970.

Norman, Hans, and Harald Runblom. *Transatlantic Connections: Nordic Migration to the New World after 1800.* Oslo, 1987.

———, eds. *Nordisk Emigrationsatlas.* 2 vols. Gävle, Sweden, 1980.

Novak, Michael. *The Rise of the Unmeltable Ethnics: Politics and Culture in the Seventies.* New York, 1975.

Olson, James Stuart. *The Ethnic Dimension in American History.* New York, 1979.

Ostendorf, Berndt, ed. *Amerikanische Gettoliteratur: Zur Literatur ethnischer, marginaler und unterdrückter Gruppen in Amerika.* Darmstadt, Germany, 1983.

Ostergren, Robert. *A Community Transplanted: The Trans-Atlantic Experience of a Swedish Immigrant Settlement in the Upper Middle West, 1835–1915.* Madison, Wis., 1988.

Øverland, Orm. "Ole Edvart Rølvaag and Giants in the Earth: A Writer between Two Countries." *American Studies in Scandinavia* 13 (1981): 35–45.

Paulson, Kristoffer F. "Berdahl Family History and Rölvaag's Immigrant Trilogy." *Norwegian-American Studies* 27 (1977): 55–76.

Peterson, Brent Orlyn. "Popular Narratives and the Constitution of Ethnic Identity: Literature and Community in *Die Abendschule.*" Ph.D. diss., University of Minnesota, 1989.

Plax, Martin. "Towards a Redefinition of Ethnic Politics." *Ethnicity* 3 (1976): 9–33.

Pochmann, Henry A. "The Mingling of Tongues." In *Literary History of the United States,* Vol. 2. Edited by Robert E. Spiller et al. New York, 1948.

Qualey, Carlton C. *Norwegian Settlement in the United States.* Northfield, Minn., 1938.

Rasmussen, Janet. *New Land, New Lives: Scandinavian Immigrants to the Pacific Northwest.* Seattle, Wash., 1993.

Reigstad, Paul. *Rølvaag: His Life and Art.* Lincoln, Nebr., 1972.

Reilly, John M. "Criticism of Ethnic Literature: Seeing the Whole Story." *MELUS* 5:1 (Spring 1978): 2–13.

Rice, John. *Patterns of Ethnicity in a Minnesota County, 1880–1905.* Umeå, Sweden, 1973.

Ristad, Ditlef G. "Landsmænd. Simon Johnson." *Nordmands-Forbundet* 20 (1927): 152–55.

Rodgers, Drew. *The Norwegian Immigrant Experience Depicted in the Works of Simon Johnson.* Telemark Distriktshøgskole. Skrifter 35. Bø, Norway, 1979.

Rokkan, Stein, and Derek W. Urwin, eds. *Economy, Territory, Identity: Politics of West European Peripheries.* London, 1983.

Rølvaag, Ole Edvart. *Amerika-breve.* Minneapolis, 1912. Published under the pseudonym of Paal Mørck.
———. *Paa glemte veie.* Minneapolis, 1914.
———. *To tullinger.* Minneapolis, 1920.
———. *Længselens baat.* Minneapolis, 1921.
———. *I de dage.* New and rev. ed. Oslo, 1977.
———. *Riket grundlægges.* New and rev. ed. Oslo, 1977.
———. *Peder Seier.* New and rev. ed. Oslo, 1977.
———. *Den signede dag.* New and rev. ed. Oslo, 1977.
Ronen, Dov. *The Quest for Self-Determination.* New Haven, Conn., 1979.
Rønnevik, Hans. *100 procent.* Carlisle, Minn., 1926.
Royce, Anya Peterson. *Ethnic Identity: Strategies of Diversity.* Bloomington, Ind., 1982.
Runblom, Harald, and Dag Blanck, eds. *Scandinavia Overseas: Patterns of Cultural Transformation in North America and Australia.* Uppsala, Sweden, 1982.
Runblom, Harald, and Hans Norman, eds. *From Sweden to America: A History of the Migration.* Minneapolis and Uppsala, Sweden, 1976.
Schach, Paul, ed. *Languages in Conflict: Linguistic Acculteration on the Great Plains.* Lincoln, Nebr., 1980.
Schultz, April. "'The Pride of the Race Had Been Touched': The 1925 Norse-American Centennial and Ethnic Identity." *Norwegian-American Studies* 33 (1992): 267–307.
———. *Ethnicity on Parade: Inventing the Norwegian American through Celebration.* Amherst, Mass., 1994.
Seller, Maxine. *To Seek America: A History of Ethnic Life in the United States.* Englewood Cliffs, N.J., 1988.
Semmingsen, Ingrid. *Veien mot vest. Utvandringen fra Norge til Amerika.* 2 vols. Oslo, 1942 and 1950.
Semmingsen, Ingrid, and Per Sejersted, eds. *Scando-Americana: Papers on Scandinavian Emigration to the United States.* Oslo, 1980.
Simonson, Harold. *Prairies Within: The Tragic Trilogy of Ole Rölvaag.* Seattle, Wash., 1987.
Skårdal, Dorothy Burton. *The Divided Heart: Scandinavian Immigrant Experience through Literary Sources.* Lincoln, Nebr., 1974.
———. "Hard 'Facts' and 'Soft' Sources: Literature as Historical Source Material?" *American Studies in Scandinavia* 16 (1984): 72–80.
Skårdal, Dorothy Burton, and Ingeborg R. Kongslien, eds. *Essays on Norwegian-American Literature and History.* Oslo, 1986.
Skarstedt, Ernst. *Pennfäktare. Svensk-amerikanska författare och tidningsmän.* Stockholm, 1930.

Smith, Anthony D. *The Ethnic Revival in the Modern World.* Cambridge, 1981.

———, ed. *Ethnicity and Nationalism.* Leiden, Netherlands, 1992.

Snyder, Louis, ed. *The Dynamics of Nationalism.* Princeton, N.J., 1964.

Soike, Lowell. *Norwegian Americans and the Politics of Dissent, 1880–1924.* Northfield, Minn., 1991.

Sollors, Werner. *Beyond Ethnicity: Consent and Descent in American Culture.* New York, 1986.

———, ed. *The Invention of Ethnicity.* New York, 1989.

Stein, Howard, and Robert Hill. *The Ethnic Imperative: Examining the New White Ethnic Movement.* University Park, Pa., 1977.

Steinberg, Stephen. *The Ethnic Myth: Race, Ethnicity and Class in America.* Boston, 1981.

Stern, Stephen, and John A. Cicala. *Creative Ethnicity: Symbols and Strategies of Contemporary Ethnic Life.* Logan, Utah, 1991.

Stone, John, ed. *Race, Ethnicity, and Social Change.* North Scituate, Mass., 1977.

Thernstrom, Stephan, ed. *Harvard Encyclopaedia of American Ethnic Groups.* Cambridge, Mass., 1980.

Thorson, Gerald. "America is not Norway: The Story of the Norwegian-American Novel." Ph.D. diss., Columbia University, 1957.

———, ed. *Ole Rølvaag: Artist and Cultural Leader.* Northfield, Minn., 1975.

Tonkin, Elizabeth, Maryon McDonald, and Malcolm Chapman, eds. *History and Ethnicity.* London, 1989.

Trommler, Frank, and Joseph McVeigh, eds. *America and the Germans.* 2 vols. Philadelphia, 1985.

Tweet, Ella Valborg. "Recollections of My Father, O. E. Rølvaag." *Minnesota English Journal* 8 (Winter 1972): 4–14.

Van den Berghe, Pierre. *The Ethnic Phenomenon.* Westport, Conn., 1987.

Vecoli, Rudolph J. "Return to the Melting Pot: Ethnicity in the United States in the Eighties." *Journal of Ethnic History* (Fall 1985): 7–20.

———. "From *The Uprooted* to *The Transplanted*: The Writing of American Immigration History, 1951–1989." In *From Melting Pot to Multiculturalism,* ed. Valeria G. Lerda, 25–53. Rome, 1991.

Vecoli, Rudolph, and Suzanne Sinke, eds. *A Century of European Migrations, 1830–1930.* Urbana, Ill., 1991.

Waldmann, Günter. *Theorie und Didaktik der Trivialliteratur.* Munich, 1973.

Warning, Rainer, ed. *Rezeptionsästhetik: Theorie und Praxis.* Munich, 1975.

Waters, Mary. *Ethnic Options: Choosing Identities in America.* Berkeley, Calif., 1990.

Wefald, Jon. *A Voice of Protest: Norwegians in American Politics, 1890–1917.* Northfield, Minn., 1971.

Wheeler, Thomas, ed. *The Immigrant Experience: The Anguish of Becoming American.* New York, 1972.

White, Hayden. *Tropics of Discourse: Essays in Cultural Criticism.* Baltimore, 1978.

Winter, Sophus K. "Moberg and a New Genre for the Emigrant Novel." *Scandinavian Studies* 34 (1962): 170–82.

Wist, Johannes, ed. *Norsk Amerikanernes Festskrift 1914.* Decorah, Iowa, 1914.

Wyman, Mark. *Immigrants in the Valley: Irish, Germans, and Americans in the Upper Mississippi Country, 1830–1860.* Chicago, 1984.

Yans-McLaughlin, Virginia, ed. *Immigration Reconsidered.* New York, 1990.

Zempel, Solveig. "Language Use in the Novels of Johannes B. Wist: A Study in Bilingualism in Literature." Ph.D. diss., University of Minnesota, 1980.

———. *In Their Own Words: Letters from Norwegian Immigrants.* Minneapolis, 1991.

Zyla, Wolodymyr, and Wendell M. Aycock, eds. *Ethnic Literatures since 1776: The Many Voices of America.* 2 vols. Lubbock, Tex., 1978.

Index

African-Americans, 58, 133
Ager, Waldemar: on American identity, 98, 101; and assimilation, 32, 41, 43, 80, 85, 98, 99; as author, 24, 27, 40, 43, 107, 131, 132–33; on education, 85, 86; and ethnonationalism, 100, 130; and German-Americans, 104; on intergenerational relations, 93–95; on the language question, 26, 84, 85, 86, 87; life of, 31; on the Lutheran Church, 90, 91, 127; on the melting pot, 80, 105; and names, 88; and the parameters of activism, 137, 138; as reviewer, 116, 119; as seen by reviewers, 111–12; and the temperance movement, 31, 134; on the transatlantic relationship, 103
America: attraction of, 66; images of, 100–102
America Not Discovered by Columbus, 25
American Indians, 38, 121, 124
American identity. *See* Americanism
Americanism: definition of, 101, 103, 135–36; interpretation of, 120, 121, 122
Americanization: desirability of, 85, 98; interpretation of, 111, 112, 115, 122–23; of native-born Americans, 122; during World War I, 12, 126
Amerika-breve, 105, 131
Anderson, Rasmus B., 25
Anglicization, 26, 65, 89, 91, 112, 121, 126
Anglo-Americans: as American mainstream, 16, 24, 29, 111; attitudes toward immigrants, 41, 64, 66
Anglo-Saxons, 124, 125
Armenian-Americans, 126
Aschehoug, 108, 135
assimilation: among American-born generations, 12; definition of, 15–16, 99; experience of, 130; necessity of, 105, 118
Augsburg Publishing House, 107, 108
Augsburg Seminary, 56
Augustana Academy, 69

Bergljot, 48
Bible, 74, 75, 85, 91, 92
Bismarck, Otto von, 61, 67, 89
Bjørnson, Bjørnstjerne, 48, 90, 127
Boelhower, William, 22, 23
Boyesen, Hjalmar Hjorth, 25
Britain, 53, 97
Buslett, Ole Amundsen, 112
bygdelag, 19, 98

Canetti, Elias, 124
Canton, South Dakota, 28, 69
Carlisle, Minnesota, 56
Catechism, 86
Catholics, 92, 104, 125, 131–32. *See also* Lutheran Church: attitudes toward Catholics in; *Peder Seier* and *Den signede dag*: Catholics and the Catholic Church in
centennial: of 1814 Eidsvoll Constitution, 11, 48; of Norwegian immigration, 11, 12
Chicago, 31, 37, 125
Colcord, Lincoln, 24
Columbus, Christopher, 25, 124
Conzen, Kathleen Neils, 17
Coolidge, Calvin, 11, 125
cultural pluralism, 100, 125–26, 130, 138. *See also* preservationism

Danish-Americans, 12, 129
Decorah-Posten, 19, 44, 111, 113, 115, 117, 118
de Francesco, Scott, 133
Den signede dag. See Peder Seier and *Den signede dag*

Democrats, 58
didactic fiction, 47, 51, 54–55, 111, 114, 134. See also literature: and politics
Dos Passos, John, 23
Duluth Skandinav, 113, 115, 117, 128
Duun, Olaf, 117

Eau Claire, Wisconsin, 28, 31
education: in American public schools, 19, 89; in Norwegian-American parochial schools, 19, 86, 90; Norwegian language in, 85, 89, 90
Elster, Kristian, 118
emigration: benefits of, 106; price of, 105–6, 115; reasons for, 66
Eriksson, Leif, 123
Et geni, 44
ethnic group. See ethnicity; ethnic minorities
ethnic literature: analysis of, 20, 22, 28–30, 83–84, 131; authors of, 26–27; definition of, 20, 22–24; and ethnic rivalry, 24; between home and host country, 135; and *Ideengeschichte,* 139; and politics, 21, 24; and style, 134
ethnic minorities, 48, 66, 85
ethnic mythology: Germanic, 124, 125; Irish-American, 123; Mayflower in, 123; Scandinavian, 123–24, 125
ethnic pride, 17, 117, 137
ethnicity: American expressions of, 15, 129; definition of, 15, 16–18; and ideology, 123; interpretation of, 98–100, 122; and literary form, 23; and religion, 126–29; and territory, 121; philiopietistic support of, 99–100; symbolic, 18, 129, 136, 138
ethnonationalism, 100, 119, 129–30
European-Americans, 15, 16, 17–18, 125, 136

Fallitten paa Braastad, 44, 46, 52
Fargo, North Dakota, 28
Fishman, Joshua, 22
Folkebladet (Minneapolis), 111
Foss, Hans A., 113, 126
Fremad Publishing Company, 107
Frihetens hjem: Anglo-American attitudes toward immigrants in, 49, 54; assimilationists in, 53–54; character development in, 51–54; compatibility of ethnic and American identities in, 50–51; historical time period of, 27; immigrant generations in, 52–53; pastors in, 53; political intent of, 54–55; portrayal of Americanism in, 46, 48–49; portrayal of Germany in, 55; portrayal of Norway in, 47–48; portrayal of Populism in, 48, 52, 53; readership of, 107–8; reviews of, 113–14; World War I in, 49

Gade, F. G., 111
Gans, Herbert, 18
Geertz, Clifford, 16
German state in America, 121
German-Americans: attitudes toward, 104, 125, 126; as a comparison to Norwegian-Americans, 29; and cultural preservationism, 120–21, 129; measures against, 31–32; religious conditions among, 128
Germany: attitudes toward, 31, 96, 97, 104, 124; national character in, 124, 125
Giants in the Earth, 24, 70, 72, 82, 115, 116
Glazer, Nathan, 17, 22
Gordon, Milton, 15, 16
Grand Forks, North Dakota, 44
Grieg, Edvard, 48
Gronna (Grønna), Asle, 60, 63, 96, 97
Gudbrandsdal, 44
Guttmann, Allen, 22
Gvåle, Gudrun Hovde, 107

Haakon VII, King of Norway, 11
Hansen, Carl G. O., 111, 128
Hansen, Marcus Lee, 136
Hassel, Nicolai Severin, 25
Haugen, Einar, 115, 131
Haugen, Kristine, 115
Haugesund Dagblad, 56
Heitmann, John, 113, 115, 117
Helgeland, 70
historiography: and literature, 21; the nature of, 20–21; and the social sciences, 21
Holvik, J. A., 116
husmenn, 44

Ibsen, Henrik, 98
Iceland, 77, 79, 124

INDEX

Icelanders, 136–37
Ideengeschichte, 139
immigrant generations: Beret and Peder as prototypes of, 116; different attitudes of, 93–95; distribution of, 11, 25; and ethnic consciousness, 18, 25; and ethnic literature, 23; and language use, 94; Hansen's law of, 136; relationship between, 87, 93–95
immigrant literature. *See* ethnic literature
immigration quotas, 12
immigration restrictions, 11, 12
intermarriage, 16, 41, 92, 118, 136
Iowa, 12
Irish-Americans, 99, 104, 123
Isaacs, Harold, 16, 17
Italian-Americans, 124

Jewish-Americans, 22, 104, 123, 126, 133
Johnson, James Weldon, 133
Johnson, Simon: as author, 27, 47, 51, 52, 53, 55, 79, 107, 131, 133, 134, 138; and German-Americans, 97, 104, 126; on identity, 99, 122; life of, 44; and names, 88–89; on Populism, 95–96; on the price of emigration, 105; as seen by reviewers, 110, 112–14; and the temperance movement, 55, 134; and World War I, 101–2

Kallen, Horace, 123
Kensington runestone, 123
Kirchendeutsche, 129
Klein, Marcus, 22
Kloss, Heinz, 127, 128, 129
Kongslien, Ingeborg, 131
Kristus for Pilatus, 110
Kvartalskrift, 31
Kvinnen og Hjemmet, 108

La Follette, Robert M., 60, 96
language retention: Danish, 12; Norwegian, 12, 65; Swedish, 12
literature: as escape, 138; and ethnicity, 15, 20, 22, 137, 138; as historical source material, 20–21, 29–30, 83–84, 93, 106, 116, 117–18, 119, 130–35, 139; and politics, 15, 20, 54–55, 82, 88, 106, 107, 108, 111, 114, 116, 117, 119, 130, 134, 137, 138, 139

Lovoll, Odd, 128
loyalism campaign, 12, 40, 65, 103
Lutheran Church: attitudes toward Catholics in, 92, 131–32; Norwegian culture in, 19, 90–92, 127; Norwegian language use in, 12, 86, 87, 90–93, 127–28, 129; and Norwegian-American ethnicity, 18, 90–93; Norwegian-American members of, 128; upbringing in, 131
Lutheran Church-Missouri Synod, 127, 128
Lutheraneren (Minneapolis), 113, 117, 128
Lutherans. *See* Lutheran Church

Manitoba, 136
Mead, Margaret, 122
melting pot, 41, 118, 123; assessment of, 43, 80, 104–6; definition of, 80, 112
Minneapolis Tidende, 19, 111, 115, 118
Minnesota, 12, 28, 56, 61, 69, 70, 97, 123
Montana, 56
Moynihan, Daniel P., 17, 22

names, 88–89, 125
National Origins Act, 12
Nelson, Knute, 97
New Englanders, 101
New York Times, 135
newspapers: Norwegian-American, 11, 19, 25, 31, 98, 107–19, 137; Scandinavian-American, 12
Nonpartisan League (NPL). *See* Populism; *100 procent:* Populism in
Nordisk Tidende (Brooklyn), 56, 108, 115, 118
Nordmands-Forbundet (publication), 111
Norgesposten (New York), 115
Normanden (Grand Forks, North Dakota), 44, 116
North Dakota, 12, 28, 44, 46, 47, 48, 58, 60, 61, 63, 66, 97
Northfield, Minnesota, 28, 70, 108
Norway, 11, 44, 56, 84, 86, 122; affinity to, 68, 100, 113; images of, 100, 102–3, 117; immigrants in, 135; knowledge of, 67, 89; publishing of Norwegian-American literature in, 108, 137; reception of Norwegian-American literature in, 111, 115, 117–18, 129, 131, 135; return to, 68, 106; transfer of cus-

toms from, 102; view of America in, 103
Norwegian America: concept of, 121, 130, 139; heartland of, 28; history of, 11–15
Norwegian language in America, 84–88; influence of English on, 67; measures against, 32; retention of, 12; speakers of, 12
Norwegian Lutheran Church in America, 12, 18. *See also* Lutheran Church
Norwegian Society of America (Det Norske Selskab i Amerika), 27, 31, 44, 56, 114
Norwegian-American Historical Association, 19, 26, 70
Norwegian-American intellectuals: and the average immigrant, 42–43, 132–33; and ethnic literature, 15, 20; limited success of, 138; and names, 88–89; personal goals of, 134, 137, 138; and preservationism, 16, 28, 30, 130
Norwegian-American literature: the duration of, 15, 24, 27, 114, 138; and ethnic pride, 117, 137, 138; leading figures of, 27; literary criticism of, 110; reviews of, 110, 114; sales figures of, 107–8; and the temperance movement, 134
Norwegian-Americans: number of, 11, 70, 107; relationship to Anglo-Americans, 103, 121, 125; relationship to German-Americans, 126; relationship to Norwegians, 100, 103
Novak, Michael, 22

odalsrett, 102
100 procent: Anglo-American attitudes toward immigrants in, 58, 64, 65, 66; assimilation in, 64, 65; assimilationists in, 58; compatibility of ethnic and American identities in, 57; German-Americans in, 58, 60, 64, 67; Germany in, 57, 60, 62; historical time period of, 27; immigrant generations in, 60; the loyalism campaign in, 60–61, 62, 63, 64, 65, 67; the Lutheran Church in, 62, 66; names in, 57, 61; the Norwegian language in, 65; Norwegian-American associations in, 61–62, 67; pastors in, 58, 60, 61–62, 64, 67; Populism in, 57, 61, 63, 66; preservationists in, 64–65; readership of, 107–8; reasons for emigration in, 66; reception of, 114; remigration in, 63–64, 67; World War I in, 56, 60, 62, 63, 64

Paa drikkeondets konto, 31
Paa veien til smeltepotten: the Anglo-American view of immigrants in, 40, 41; assessment of the melting pot in, 40, 43; cultural role of the Lutheran Church in, 42; historical setting of, 27, 31; immigrant generations in, 32, 34–35, 37, 38, 41–42; the Norwegian language in, 34; the Norwegian-American relationship to Anglo-Americans in, 32, 35, 38, 39; portrayal of assimilation in, 41; portrayal of New Englanders in, 36, 39, 41; portrayal of pastors in, 34, 39; price of emigration in, 37–38, 40, 43; pride in Norway in, 36; readership of, 107–8; reviews of, 111–12; temperance organizations in, 36
Peder Seier and *Den signede dag*: Anglo-American attitudes toward immigrants in, 72; assessment of the melting pot in, 80; Catholics and the Catholic Church in, 73, 75–78, 80, 81; character development in, 79–82; education in, 72; historical time period of, 27; immigrant generations in, 79; interethnic marriage in, 74; interethnic relations in, 72, 73; Irish-Americans in, 73, 78, 80, 81; the Jewish example in, 77; Lutherans and the Lutheran Church in, 73, 75–78, 81; the Norwegian language in, 72, 74, 79, 80; pastors in, 74, 77; preservationists in, 77, 79; readership of, 108; resilience of ethnic identity in, 81; reviews of, 115–19
Pennsylvania, 120
philiopietism, 99–100
Populism, 95–96
preservationism, 112, 120; and activist literature, 99, 119, 133; and Americanization, 26, 108–10; concept of, 121, 123, 129; and the Lutheran Church, 128; motivation for, 130, 137

Rædselsdagene, et norsk billede fra indianerkrigen, 25

INDEX

Reform (Eau Claire, Wisconsin), 31, 107, 111, 116, 117, 119
religion: and ethnicity, 90–93, 126–29; and the temperance movement, 134. *See also under individual denominations*
Republicans, 57, 78, 95, 104
remigration, 68, 106
Restauration, vessel, 24
Rolvaag, Karl, 70
Rølvaag, Ole Edvart: as author, 24–25, 27, 107, 108; on education, 89, 90; and ethnonationalism, 99, 100, 129–30, 135; on interethnic relations, 103–4; on the language question, 26, 84, 85, 86, 87; life of, 69; and literary style, 79–80, 82, 88, 131; and New Englanders, 101; and the parameters of literary activism, 135, 137; on politics, 95–96; on the price of emigration, 105–6; on religion, 91–92, 131; as reviewer, 110, 113–14, 134; and Scandinavian-American mythology, 125; as seen by reviewers, 115–19
Rønnevik, Hans: on Americanism, 65, 66, 98; and German-Americans, 67, 97, 104, 126; language use of, 67; life of, 56; and names, 88; on pastors, 91, 92; on Populism, 96; as a preservationist author, 27, 83; and publishing, 107, 114; and remigration, 68, 106; and the wartime atmosphere, 67–68, 92, 102
Runblom, Harald, 26, 27

Sandburg, Carl, 23
Saxton, Eugene, 131
Scandia (Chicago), 115
Scandinavian-Americans, 12, 22, 126
Shils, Edward, 16
Skandinaven (Chicago), 19, 78, 114, 115, 117
Skårdal, Dorothy Burton, 22, 23, 25
Skørdalsvold, J. J., 111, 113

slavery, 122, 125
Slavic-Americans, 125, 126
social sciences, 21
Sollors, Werner, 17, 22, 23, 122, 133
Sons of Norway, 20, 98, 129
South Dakota, 28, 56, 69, 70
St. Brendan, 123
St. Olaf College, 24, 69, 90
Stenholt, Lars A., 24
Stockenström, Göran, 26
Swedish-Americans, 12, 26, 29, 58, 129

temperance movement, 31, 55, 134
Tendenz, 133
Teutonic myth, 124, 125
Turks, 135

Ukrainian-Americans, 125
Undset, Sigrid, 124
Undstad, Lyder, 116
United States census, 11, 12, 107, 136
University of Oslo, 69

van den Berghe, Pierre, 17
Vecoli, Rudolph, 17
Ved Lampelys, 56
Veien til Golden Gate, 112
Vereinsdeutsche, 129
Vikings, 50, 98, 123, 124

Washington Posten (Seattle), 111
Washington, George, 61, 89, 122
White, Hayden, 21
Wicke, Victor G., 133
Wist, Johannes, 27
World War I: and Americanization, 12, 40, 70, 89, 125–26; assessment of, 96–97, 101–2; and names, 89, 125; Norwegian-American attitudes toward, 97; the Scandinavian-American experience of, 126; the societal atmosphere of, 27, 31, 125

Zangwill, Israel, 123

CHICAGO PUBLIC LIBRARY
SULZER REGIONAL
4455 N. LINCOLN AVE. 60625

THE CHICAGO PUBLIC LIBRARY

FORM 19